From Torah to Kabbalah

# From Torah to Kabbalah

*A Basic Introduction to the
Writings of Judaism*

R. C. Musaph-Andriesse

New York
OXFORD UNIVERSITY PRESS
1982

Translated by John Bowden from the Dutch
*Wat na de Tora kwam, Rabbijnse literatuur van
Tora tot Kabbala*
Published 1973 by Uitgeverij Ten Have bv, Baarn, Holland.
© 1973 Uitgeverij Ten Have bv, Baarn, Holland

Translation © John Bowden 1981

First Published in England, 1981,
by SCM Press

First Published in the United States, 1982,
by Oxford University Press

Library of Congress Cataloging in Publication Data

Musaph-Andriesse, R. C.
      From Torah to Kabbalah.

      Translation of: Wat na de Tora kwam.
      Bibliography: p.
      Includes index.
      1. Rabbinical literature—History and
criticism. I. Title.
BM496.5.M8513    1982      296.1      81-18964
ISBN 0-19-520364-X                    AACR2

Printing (last digit):  9 8 7 6 5 4 3 2 1

Printed in the United States of America

# Contents

# Preface

This book is intended for those who are interested in the Bible and would also like to increase their knowledge of the Jewish literature that was written after the Bible.

Post-biblical literature, which arose out of the Torah, is usually called rabbinic literature. The very extensive material is not accessible to many people because it is largely untranslated, and requires a thorough knowledge of Hebrew and Aramaic to be understood. However, questions about it often arise. What is the Talmud and when was it written? What is a midrash? What is the Shulḥan ʿAruk? In the following pages I shall discuss the main works of rabbinic literature and sketch out their background. I have covered the period from the Torah to the Middle Ages. Important trends like Hasidism, the Enlightenment, Liberalism and perhaps even Zionism fall outside the compass of this book.

I hope that I have succeeded in clarifying some of the confusion that can be caused by this literature. Anyone who wants to pursue their reading further will find an extensive bibliography at the end of the book.

# The Spelling of Hebrew and Aramaic Terms

Since Hebrew and Aramaic use a different alphabet from the one with which we are familiar, proper names, titles and other words have to be transliterated if those who know no Hebrew or Aramaic are to be able to pronounce them. This leads to all sorts of minor problems, largely caused because many Hebrew letters do not have equivalents in English. Over the course of time different systems of transliteration have developed, so that the same term can become almost unrecognizable as the reader moves from one reference book to another: *b* can become *v*; *k* can become *q* or *c*; *ḥ* can be written as it is in fact pronounced, *ch*; signs like ' (representing *aleph*, a consonant which is not pronounced) and ʿ (representing *ayin*, a consonant pronounced like *ng* at the back of the throat) are sometimes included and sometimes ignored, and so on.

In an introductory book of this kind it seemed best to opt for simplicity at the cost of consistency. Some names have not, strictly speaking, been transliterated at all: Moses, Isaac, Samuel, Solomon are so well established in that form that it would be pedantic to use a more accurate form of the original. Other names and terms have become established in one form of transliteration; where that is the case, I have not altered them to bring them into line with the basic system used here. That system lacks some of the finer points of scholarly transliteration (for example, it does not mark the length of vowels); however, it should serve its purpose.

*John Bowden*

# 1 Tanach

Tanach is the usual Hebrew name for the Old Testament. The earliest Hebrew term for the Bible is *haSefarim* ('the books'). Greek-speaking Jews translated this as *ta biblia*. The Greek *biblos* or *biblion* originally denoted a scroll of papyrus, then something on which one could write, and later still the text itself. Via the Latin, the term *ta biblia* has become our word 'Bible'.

In the Middle Ages, the Jews used the designation *Miqra* a great deal. Literally, it means 'the reading'. We also find the term *sifre haQodesh* ('the holy books'), which appears in Hebrew literature from the Middle Ages on; presumably it was used in spoken language a good deal earlier.

## (a) Contents

The Tanach is made up of:
  The Torah, the Hebrew word for 'teaching, instruction'.
  The Nebiim, the Hebrew word for 'prophets'.
  The Ketubim, the Hebrew word for 'writings'.
The term Tanach is made up of the first three letters of *T*orah, *N*ebiim and *K*etubim, with vowels between to make them pronounceable as a word (in this context, following Hebrew pronunciation, the *k* softens to *ch*). Some books may use the form Tenach or Tanak. We shall come up against this fondness for using initial letters to make a new name in connection with mediaeval scholars (see p. 55 below).

The Torah comprises the following five books:
  Bereshith  = In the beginning
  Shemoth   = Names
  Wayyiqra = And he called

1

Bemidbar = In the wilderness
Debarim  = Words, things

These Hebrew names are derived from the first word with which each book opens.

The non-Hebrew names for the books are derived from the Latin translation of the Bible, which in turn borrows from the Greek; these names characterize the contents of the books. They are:

Genesis = Creation, becoming

Exodus = Departure

Leviticus = Priestly: the allusion is to the cultic (levitical) regulations and laws for priests which are dealt with in this part

Numbers (Numeri) An allusion to the census which is described in the first part of this book

Deuteronomy (Deuteronomium) = Repetition, for the second time. Deut. 17.18 in fact mentions the 'copy of the law'. The Greek translators wrongly applied this to the whole book and presented it as a 'second lawgiving'.

At the time when it came into being, the Torah did not have the central place that it would later occupy. Since the time of Ezra (c.458 BC), the Torah has been the basic law for the Jewish tradition.

Ezra, who is called *haSofer* ('the scribe', 'the scholar'), himself played an important part in making the Torah known again; in his time it had really faded into the background. Only when the Jews had returned to Jerusalem from Babylon did he succeed in making the Torah once more the central point of Jewish life. Ezra stands out as an indefatigable champion of the revival and implementation of the Torah. In the book of Ezra he is described as the man who restored the Torah to the people.

The Torah is also given a number of other names. For instance, it is spoken of as 'The Five Books of Moses'; in Hebrew we often find *ḥumash*, which literally means 'a fifth' (the Hebrew word for five is *ḥamish* or *ḥamishya*). People also talked about *ḥamishya ḥumshe torah* ('five-fifths of the Torah'). The Greek term 'Pentateuch', which is also used a great deal, means 'consisting of five parts'.

The second part of the Tanach, Nebiim, the Prophets, is divided into:

Nebiim rishonim = The Former Prophets
Nebiim aḥaronim = The Latter Prophets

The Nebiim rishonim comprise the following books (in each case transliterations of the Hebrew title follow the familiar version):

Joshua (*yehoshuʿa*)
Judges (*shofetim*)
I & II Samuel (*shemuʾel aleph* and *beth*)
I & II Kings (*melakim aleph* and *beth*)

The Nebiim aḥaronim comprise:

Isaiah (*yishʿyahu*)
Jeremiah (*irmeyahu*)
Ezekiel (*yehezqeʾl*)

Twelve Minor Prophets:
Hosea (*hosheʿa*)
Joel (*yoʿel*)
Amos (*ʿamos*)
Obadiah (*ʿobadyah*)
Jonah (*yonah*)
Micah (*mikah*)
Nahum (*nahum*)
Habakkuk (*habaqquq*)
Zephaniah (*ṣefanyah*)
Haggai (*haggay*)
Zechariah (*zekaryah*)
Malachi (*malʾaki*)

The Ketubim, the third part of the Tanach, comprises those writings which in Greek are called Hagiographa. There are twelve parts, which have little connection with one another. In the Tanach they are arranged as follows:

Psalms (*tehillim*)
Proverbs (*mishle*)
Job (*iyyob*)

Song of Songs (*shir-haShirim*)
Ruth (*ruth*)
Lamentations (*ekah*)
Preacher (*qoheleth*)
Esther (*'esther*)

These are the five Megilloth (singular *megillah* = scroll)

Daniel (*dany'el*)
Ezra (*'ezra'*)
Nehemiah (*nehemyah*)
I and II Chronicles (*dibre hayyamim aleph* and *beth*)

Together, all the books so far mentioned form the Hebrew Bible, or the Old Testament.

At this point it should be noted that the Authorized (King James) Version and subsequently all non-Catholic translations of the Old Testament, via the Septuagint and the Vulgate, have the books in a different order. In English translations the concern has been to arrange the books in accordance with their content, as follows:

| *Law* | *Historical books* | *Poetic books* | *Prophets* |
|---|---|---|---|
| Genesis | Joshua | Job | Isaiah |
| Exodus | Judges | Psalms | Jeremiah |
| Leviticus | Ruth | Proverbs | Lamentations |
| Numbers | I and II Samuel | Ecclesiastes | Ezekiel |
| Deuteronomy | I and II Kings | Song of | Daniel |
| (This order is | I and II | Songs | Hosea |
| the same as | Chronicles | | Joel |
| in the | Ezra | | Amos |
| Tanach) | Nehemiah | | Obadiah |
| | Esther | | Jonah |
| | | | Micah |
| | | | Nahum |
| | | | Habakkuk |
| | | | Zephaniah |
| | | | Haggai |
| | | | Zechariah |
| | | | Malachi |

Thus in this division the five Megilloth (Song of Songs, Ruth, Lamentations, Koheleth and Esther) are no longer together. The

4

Megilloth are short books, originally written on parchment scrolls, which were read out in the synagogue on particular days. Presumably this is why they were put in the Tanach. They are read as follows:

| | |
|---|---|
| Song of Songs | at Pesach (Passover) |
| Ruth | at Shabuoth (Pentecost) |
| Lamentations | on the 9th Ab, to recall the destruction of the Temple |
| Koheleth | at Sukkoth (Feast of Tabernacles) |
| Esther | at Purim (Feast of Lots) |

Only Esther is still really read from a scroll (Megillath Esther); the rest are read from the Tanach.

The arrangement of the Minor Prophets in the Greek translation differs slightly from that given here. The order is: Hosea, Amos, Micah, Joel, Obadiah, Jonah, Nahum – and after that it is the same.

### (i) The content of the five books of the Torah

The first book, Bereshith (Genesis), is a collection of stories about the creation of the world, the flood and the patriarchs. It ends with the story of Joseph.

The second book, Shemoth (Exodus), continues the cycle of stories. After the account of the exodus from Egypt and the wanderings in the wilderness, the character of the book changes. The giving of the Law on Mount Sinai occupies a central place. There follow a great many laws, commands and prohibitions, prescriptions and regulations.

The third book, Wayyiqra (Leviticus), chiefly deals with priestly laws and the regulations for offering sacrifices. The narrative element of the previous books is almost entirely absent.

The fourth book, Bemidbar (Numbers), is an account of events during the long stay of the Israelites in the wilderness.

The fifth and last book of the Torah, Debarim (Deuteronomy), again contains a large number of legal regulations, many of them of a social nature. Some of them also appear in Shemoth. The beginning of the book contains a number of warnings to the people, given by Moses while the people were still in the wilderness on the far bank of the Jordan, and were expecting to enter the Promised Land. The nucleus of the book is made up of legal regulations, some of which are a literal repetition of those in

5

Shemoth. The conclusion of this last book of the Torah again contains a number of warnings, along with some narratives. It also includes the famous 'Song of Moses' (ch. 32), which is regarded as one of the earliest examples of Israelite literature. The death of Moses forms the conclusion of the book Debarim and also of the Torah.

### (ii) The content of the Nebiim

The Former Prophets describes the history of Israel from the conquest of Canaan to the destruction of the Temple.

Joshua describes the conquest of Canaan and its division between the tribes. The book of Shofetim (Judges) continues the history down to the death of Samson. The book ends with an account of the outrage of Gibeah and the war against Benjamin which results from it.

The first part of Samuel tells the story of the prophet Samuel and describes the rise of Saul and David. The second part begins with the death of Saul. We then have an account of the wars waged by David against surrounding enemies, his victories and defeats.

The two parts of Melakim (Kings) deal with the period between Solomon and the destruction of the Temple in 586 BC by Nebuchadnezzar. The division of the kingdom into two parts, Israel and Judah, and their subsequent histories, appears in these books.

The Latter Prophets includes the three greatest prophets to appear in Israel: Isaiah, Jeremiah and Ezekiel. The twelve minor prophets are often regarded as one book. They were called 'minor' not because of their status but because of the size of their books. Hosea and Amos in particular were important prophets.

### (iii) The content of the Ketubim

Tehillim (Psalms) is a collection of songs of praise, thanksgiving and lamentation: there are marriage songs, songs of triumph and victory, and royal songs. Hebrew uses *tehillim* (psalms) only in the plural. For the singular, the word *mizmor* (song, accompanied on a stringed instrument) is used rather than the singular of *tehillim* (*tehillah* = song of praise). The psalms were composed at different times; it is impossible to establish their dates exactly. They vary from before the Babylonian Captivity until shortly afterwards (cf. Ps. 137: 'By the waters of Babylon'). The book of Psalms was probably completed in the second century BC. Some of the psalms are ascribed to David.

Mishle (Proverbs) is part of the wisdom literature of Israel (= *sifroth haḥokmah*). It is a collection of discourses and sayings which have a moral, convey a warning and serve to edify. Wisdom literature generally is a genre in which experience plays a major part. It was handed down from father to son. Its morality is concerned with relationships between human beings, and not between man and God. The wise man is not a prophet whose words are communicated by divine revelation; far less is he a priest, who is bound by particular cultic regulations. He is a counsellor, particularly in connection with ordinary everyday things and ordinary simple people. The wise man is trained in playing with words and ideas often in the form of a riddle, a saying, a simile or a tale. He is fond of moralizing without himself bringing out the moral. In his morality good triumphs over evil; he identifies himself with the good.

Job and Koheleth are also part of the wisdom literature of the Tanach, though there is a difference in the form of wisdom which they contain. Whereas the wisdom in Proverbs is conservative, didactic, and practical, with an optimistic undertone, in Job and Koheleth the wisdom is radical, critical, individualistic and with a pessimistic undertone.

The date of Proverbs is as uncertain as that of the Psalms. The whole collection will have been completed round about the middle of the fourth century BC. Part of the book is attributed to Solomon.

Job. Central to this book is the suffering man in confrontation with God. Job is put to the test by God, but does not lose his trust in God. He asks himself what the meaning of suffering is when a man thinks that he is innocent. He wants to rid himself of the thought that suffering is a punishment which follows sin, but in the dialogue which he has with his three friends the friends once again stress this notion of retribution very strongly indeed. Finally Job gives way to his God and says that the meaning of suffering can never be measured by human standards. The highest wisdom is expressed by Job in simple words: 'God gave. God has taken away. Praised be the name of God.' These words are still constantly repeated when the believer is confronted with the deepest suffering. It is difficult to establish the date of the book of Job.

*Shir haShirim* (Song of Songs). This collection of idyllic love songs is a marriage hymn which was presumably sung during the marriage feast, which lasted for seven days. Because of the spring-like character of the book it is read in the synagogue on the feast of Pesach (Passover).

The secular character of the book led both Jews and Christians to look for an interpretation which fitted its contents better. For Jews this is the love between God (the bridegroom) and his people (the bride); for Christians, between Jesus and his church. In all probability the Song of Songs was included in the canon as a result of this allegorical interpretation. Its date must be put round about the third century BC.

Ruth. This tale relates how Ruth, a Moabite woman, comes to be married to Boaz, an Israelite of good standing. A son is born of this marriage, who at the end of the book is said to be King David's grandfather. How far this is historically correct is highly questionable. Perhaps the author wanted to show his approval of the fact that Ruth, a non-Jewish woman, became the ancestress of David, which went against the rules forbidding mixed marriages which were announced by Ezra when the Jews returned to Jerusalem. The dating of the book would fit with this very well, since it is generally accepted that the book was written at the end of the fifth century or during the fourth century BC. The encounter between Ruth and Boaz takes place at harvest time. The fields are the background against which the story is told. For that reason the book is read in the synagogue at Shabuoth (Pentecost).

*Ekah* (Lamentations). The opening word of this collection of lamentations is *Ekah*, which means 'woe', 'alas'. On the 9th Ab (roughly our August), these lamentations were recited in the synagogue to recall the destruction of the Temple. They were probably written shortly after the fall of Jerusalem.

Koheleth. This piece of wisdom literature is a collection of aphorisms and reflections on human life and the characteristics which go to make it up. Koheleth certainly speaks of God, but the writer clearly presupposes that God is hidden from men and remains so. It has a markedly individualistic flavour. The author of Koheleth – who is not Solomon, as has just been said – probably lived around 300 BC. The name Koheleth (preacher) indicates that the allusion is to one of the spokesmen of the community. He speaks as though he were Solomon, but does not give his own name. The book is read in the synagogue at Sukkoth (The Feast of Tabernacles).

Megillath Esther. This book is an attractive account of the way in which Esther, a Jewish girl, becomes the wife of Ahasuerus, the Persian king, through her uncle Mordecai. When the Jews are threatened with extermination, she is able to save her people by interceding with the king. A lot had indicated that this was to happen on the 13th Adar. The Jewish name for the festival of which Esther is the legend is Purim, from the Babylonian word for lot = *pur*. Esther is read in the synagogue on the 14th/15th Adar (round about February/March) to recall the fact that the Jews were able to escape extermination. There are doubts about the historicity of this book; it is probably a festal legend with which particular historical events have come to be associated. The story of Esther was written in the fifth century BC, and probably took its final form round about the third or second century BC. Together with Koheleth and Shir-haShirim it is one of those books of the Tanach which were only accepted into the canon of the Old Testament after a great deal of discussion.

Daniel. This book tells the story of Daniel, who was carried off into captivity in 605 BC, together with three friends from Jerusalem. He lived at the court of the Babylonian king Nebuchadnezzar. The book falls into two main parts: the first six chapters, which are of a narrative kind; and chapters 7–12, which have an apocalyptic character. Daniel has a high reputation after he has given a skilful interpretation of a dream which Nebuchadnezzar had. In ch. 5 we read how he prophesied the coming of the Persian king Cyrus and the fall of Nebuchadnezzar by deciphering the mysterious writing on the wall. Chapter 6 contains the story of Daniel in the lions' den. The later chapters describe four of Daniel's visions. Along with Ezra, Daniel is the only book of the Tanach which is written partly in Aramaic and partly in Hebrew. It is one of the latest books of the Tanach, probably dating from 165 BC.

Ezra. This man, who was regarded as a great scholar, was an important official with the Persian government. In 538 BC the Jews were given permission by king Cyrus to return to Jerusalem. This book describes successively which of the people returned, the rebuilding of an altar in Jerusalem, and the beginning of the reconstruction of the Temple. The local inhabitants put up strong resistance against this. Darius, king of Persia, then gave orders for the work to be resumed. Ezra was subsequently given authority by the king to restore the Temple worship. In 458 BC he arrived in Jerusalem, and there discovered that the people had been intermarrying with the local inhabitants. His fierce opposition to mixed marriages – he required foreign wives to be put away – forms the conclusion to the book. By his vigorous efforts Ezra restored the Torah to the centre of Jewish life and thus played a central role in securing the continued existence of the Jewish people.

Nehemiah is a continuation of the story of Ezra. Nehemiah was originally in the service of the Persian king Artaxerxes I. When he heard of the distressing conditions obtaining in Jerusalem, he asked for permission to go there. He became governor of Judah in 444 BC. When he arrived in Jerusalem he immediately began by restoring the city walls. These were rebuilt under his leadership, a move which was extremely important for the freedom of the Jews. After returning to Persia for a while, Nehemiah set up permanent residence in Jerusalem where, like Ezra, he promulgated regulations to enforce the Torah.

The books of Ezra and Nehemiah were originally a single book. We cannot go into their complicated chronology here. Both books can be dated to about 400 BC.

*Dibre hayyamim* (Chronicles). The content of these two parts covers ground which to a large extent has already been described in Melakim (Kings). The first nine chapters consist exclusively of genealogies of the tribes of Judah, starting with Adam and Eve. The end of the book is identical with the beginning of the book of Ezra. Like Ezra and Nehemiah, the book also dates from about 400 BC. The importance of Chronicles lies more in its conception of history than in the events which it narrates, which in any case are already known to us from Kings. The author of the work probably had a particular end in view and wanted to stress the period after the exile. Temple worship is restored, Jerusalem again becomes a focal point, and the Torah is again observed, thanks to the work of Ezra and Nehemiah.

## (b) The character of the Tanach

*Torah* means teaching. The chief significance of the Torah lies in its central section, which is made up of a large number of commands and prohibitions. The orthodox Jewish tradition regards the whole of the Torah as the Law given by God to Moses on Mount Sinai. This explains why, for Judaism, the Torah is holy and unassailable.

The earliest literature of the Tanach, the Song of Deborah (Judges 5), was probably composed in the eleventh century BC. Other books, like the story of Esther, come from the fifth century BC. The Book of Daniel is even later. All the literature and the historical accounts contained in the Tanach were composed and written down in the intervening period. Scholarly research has established beyond all possible doubt that the Tanach reached its definitive form over a long period. The book Debarim (Deuteronomy) dates from about 700 BC.

Many authors played a part in the creation of the Tanach, and almost all of them are unknown to us. It is only exceptionally that any one is mentioned to us by name. This happens, for example, in the book of Jeremiah, where we discover that Jeremiah's friend Baruch wrote for him. Some of the Psalms are ascribed to David and the Proverbs to Solomon. As a rule, however, the author is not named, and this is a typical characteristic of the accounts in the Tanach. The author is unimportant: he is secondary to the end in view, namely, to record a part of history for future generations. The author's own reputation or glory is made secondary to this.

## (c) Translations of the Bible

Even in the time of Ezra, Hebrew was no longer the principal language of the Jewish people. It had been replaced by Aramaic. So reading the Torah in the language in which it was originally written, Hebrew, led to difficulties: people no longer understood what they heard. At that stage people already began to make a translation of the Tanach into Aramaic. The translation of the Torah was read out after the Hebrew text. This kind of Aramaic translation is called a *targum* (the modern Hebrew word for 'translate' is *tirgim*). The most important Targumim are the Targum

11

Onqelos on the Torah, named after Onqelos, a pupil of Rabbi Aqiba, and the Targum Jonathan on the prophets. Both translations were probably made in Palestine; Onqelos already in the second or third century AD, and Jonathan rather later. The final versions were produced in Babylon about the fifth century AD.

These Targumim are still used a great deal in the study of the Tanach. The Targum Onqelos gives an almost literal translation of the Torah. In addition to these two Targumim, I should also mention another Targum on the Tanach known as the Jerusalem Targum, which is also called Pseudo-Jonathan.

The most important translation of the Tanach is the Greek Septuagint, which means 'the seventy'. This translation is often indicated by the Roman numeral LXX. The legend is that seventy people were involved in the translation. A great many Jews were already living in Egypt in the third century BC, particularly in Alexandria. They, too, no longer knew Hebrew and so a Greek translation was made to ensure that they were familiar with the contents of the Tanach (about 260 BC). This Septuagint was of considerable importance, since it was the way in which the non-Jewish world came to know the Bible. It still enjoys great authority among scholars because of the evidence it provides for the biblical text and the many ways in which it helps to explain the original Hebrew.

Other Greek translations, which were made later, include those by Aquila (some think that he is identical with Onqelos, whom I have already mentioned, but this has not been proved), Theodotion and Symmachus. Aquila (c. AD 130) translated the Hebrew text very slavishly; Theodotion (c. AD 150) deviates more from the Hebrew text because his work is based on the Septuagint, and Symmachus (c. AD 200) made a new Greek translation of the Bible. Because so many different translations appeared one after the other, Origen (184–253) collected them together in a book which had six columns, the so-called Hexapla. This contains, side by side: the Hebrew text, the Hebrew text in Greek letters, Aquila, Symmachus, Septuagint, Theodotion. Almost nothing has survived of this work, which was produced about AD 230.

A Syriac translation, the Peshitta or Peshitto (= the simple, viz., translation), was made in the second century AD. This translation was produced in a Christian community in North Syria.

A Latin translation was also made in the second century AD,

going back to the Septuagint: the *Vetus Latina* (= Old Latin, viz. translation) or *Itala*. It is a collection of Latin translations. To improve this, in AD 400 Jerome made a new translation which for the most part was made from both Greek and Hebrew texts, the so-called Vulgate (= the common, viz. translation). The Psalms in the Vulgate are still in the Old Latin translation. Since the ninth century this Vulgate has displaced the *Vetus Latina*, and was long regarded as normative by the Roman Catholic church.

Saadya Gaon (882–942) was the first to translate the Bible into Arabic, in the tenth century. Over the course of the centuries, countless translations of the Bible have appeared in every language.

### (d) The Masoretes

The Tanach was originally written without vowels. Hebrew is a typical consonantal language, i.e. it is written solely in consonants, to which vowels are supplied. Furthermore, no punctuation marks are used. One discovers what vowels are used by hearing words pronounced; this is fully in accord with the character of the Torah, which is often delivered by heart. The technique of learning things off by heart in this way was developed to a considerable degree. We find the same thing with the Arabs, who can recite the text of the Koran by rote.

As knowledge of the Tanach steadily decreased, because Aramaic replaced Hebrew as the main language, there was a risk that the language would become corrupted, and eventually be lost. So a system of punctuation was introduced. Vowels were added (in Hebrew, *nikkud*), punctuation marks, and later also notation and divisions into paragraphs. This work was done by the Masoretes (the Hebrew verb *masar* means 'hand down, pass on, transmit'). Furthermore, the constant copying of the text, which of course was done by hand, had led to the introduction of mistakes, which the Masoretes sought to eliminate.

The *soferim* (= the scribes) were the people involved in constantly copying the Tanach, because of their knowledge of it. To begin with, a *sofer* was someone who had this great knowledge of the Torah in general, a scholar. Later the word came above all to denote someone who was particularly occupied in copying the text.

The Masoretes, who worked in different schools, compared all possible texts and arrived at a standard text, the so-called Masoretic text. The Masora collects together everything that goes with the text of the Tanach but is not an integral part of it. The hundreds of notes which make it up are put in the margin and divided into two groups: the Masora Parva (the little Masora) and the Masora Magna (the great Masora).

The Masora Parva consists of short notes which are often abbreviated in accordance with a consistent system. Small circles or stars in the text indicate the relevant notes in the margin. The most important notes in the Masora Parva are the so-called *qere*, Aramaic for 'what is read', and *ketib*, Aramaic for 'what is written'. These notes indicate respectively either that the word written differs from the word pronounced, or that the word pronounced differs from the word written.

The Masoretes worked in both Babylonia and in Palestine. There were two schools in Tiberias in Palestine, one of them under the leadership of the family of Ben Asher, and the other under the direction of the family of Ben Naphthali. They were keen rivals, but in the end the Masoretic text of Ben Asher became the standard text of the Tanach. This text was established in 1008 or 1009. The original manuscript is in the possession of the Public Library of Leningrad, and is called the Codex Leningrad (MS B 19a). As well as this, there is the Codex Aleppo, which dates from 930 and is also ascribed to Ben Asher. From the fourteenth century on, the manuscript was stored away in a synagogue in Aleppo, but it is now in Jerusalem. Jerusalem University is preparing a new critical edition of the Tanach on the basis of this manuscript. M. Goshen-Gottstein thinks that the Aleppo Codex was used by Maimonides in the preparation of his edition of the text, because this codex must have been in Egypt (from the eleventh to the fourteenth century) before it was taken to Aleppo.

Both these codices, the Codex Leningrad and the Codex Aleppo, go back to a different original which was vocalized and provided with Masora by the last scholar of the Ben Asher family, Aaron ben Moshe ben Asher. His father, Moshe ben Asher, is credited with having produced the so-called Codex of the

14

Prophets, which was made in Tiberias and is now in the possession of the Qaraite synagogue in Cairo. This is the earliest known codex of the whole of the prophets. For a long time, different versions of these Masoretic texts continued to be used side by side, including those of the Ben Naphthali family.

The first printed Hebrew Bible appeared in Venice in 1525, and is known as the Bombergiana. The text of the Codex Leningrad is used in third edition of the *Biblia Hebraica* (*BHK*[3], 1937), edited by R. Kittel and P. Kahle, and its successor, *Biblia Hebraica Stuttgartensis* (BHS, 1976/77), edited by K. Elliger and W. Rudolph, with many collaborators.

# 2   The Canon

The word canon is the Latinized form of the Greek word *kanon* ('measure, rod'), which in turn is derived from Semitic languages. The Hebrew *kane* means 'measure', 'rod', 'tube'. The meaning standard, or measure, in a general sense comes via the Greek; from the fourth century AD the word is used specifically for the list of the sacred books making up the Bible. Subsequently the term came also to be applied to the books which had authority because they appeared on this list.

(*a*) The process of canonization

As far as we can see, the Torah was already a complete entity by about 300 BC. The prophetic books, too, will also have been more or less complete by 200 BC. Further changes will certainly have been made, but by and large the form and content will have been established. The greatest difficulties arose over the canonization of the Writings, at least a part of which were composed at a later stage. There was considerable doubt about the sacred character of some of these books, like Esther, Ecclesiastes and the Song of Songs. The rabbis who had to decide whether or not to accept them into the canon spent a long time discussing them. They looked for a guideline, but it is still uncertain precisely what standards they applied. When they finally had to come to a definitive conclusion, round about AD 100, the rabbis probably accepted without further question the Torah and all the literature which had been produced before 500 BC; they constantly kept changing their minds about the rest. The final decision was left to the school of Yavneh (the Greek Jamnia), which was the spiritual centre of the Jews from the fall of Jerusalem in AD 70 to about 135. Once the canon had been definitively established, no further books were either added or rejected.

The consequence of this was that a number of important books and writings which had been composed in a Jewish milieu and had been written in Hebrew or Aramaic were left out of the canon. These books are called the apocrypha ('the hidden books') and the pseudepigrapha (a term used to indicate that they are attributed to someone who is not really the author). In fact some of the apocrypha might just as well be called pseudepigrapha. In Hebrew the apocrypha are called the *sefarim hitsonim*.

## (b) Apocrypha and Pseudepigrapha

These, then, are the terms used to denote books which were not included in the canon. The books concerned were composed in the period between the Old and the New Testaments, in the second or first centuries BC. The Septuagint contains a number of books which are not included in the Hebrew Bible, and is therefore more extensive. The Protestant churches have followed the Jewish tradition, and regard the books of the Hebrew Bible as canonical. The Roman Catholic Church has followed the Septuagint, and regards most of the books contained in the Septuagint but not in the Hebrew Bible as deutero-canonical; the Septuagint is accepted as authoritative.

The Protestant churches have also made a further distinction, between Apocrypha and Pseudepigrapha; the Roman Catholic church calls the books termed Pseudepigrapha by the Protestant church Apocrypha, and has no Pseudepigrapha.

The books in question are classified as follows:

*Apocrypha in the Protestant churches = Deutero-canonical books in the Roman Catholic Church*

Tobit (Tobias)   (originally written in Hebrew or Aramaic in the second century BC)

Judith   (originally written in Hebrew, presumably in the second century BC)

The Wisdom of Solomon   (composed in Hellenistic circles about the first century BC)

Baruch   (presumably from the first century BC)

17

The Letter of Jeremiah

I and II Maccabees   (the first written in Hebrew, the second in Greek, both during the second century BC)

Additions to the Book of Daniel   (date uncertain)

Additions to the Book of Esther   (presumably from the first century BC)

The Wisdom of Jesus Sirach   (written in Hebrew in the second century BC)

*Apocrypha in both the Protestant churches and the Roman Catholic Church*

III and IV Maccabees   (first century BC)

III and IV Ezra (Esdras)   (second century BC)

The Prayer of Manasseh   (date uncertain)

*Apocrypha in the Roman Catholic Church = Pseudepigrapha in the Protestant churches*

These books were written predominantly in a Jewish milieu at the end of the Old Testament period. They comprise:

The Letter of Aristeas   (end of the second century BC)

Jubilees   (originally written in Hebrew; end of the second century BC)

The Testaments of the Twelve Patriarchs   (originally written in Hebrew or Aramaic; second or first century BC)

I Enoch   (about 165 BC)

The Psalms of Solomon   (originally in Hebrew; about 50 BC)

The Assumption of Moses   (the beginning of the Christian era)

The Ascension of Isaiah   (the beginning of the Christian era)

The Apocalypse of Baruch   (II Baruch, AD 50–100)

The Sibylline Books   (round about the beginning of the Christian era)

The Damascus Document   (originally written in Hebrew; second or first century BC).

For the most part, the apocryphal books are anonymous; the authors are unknown. The number of apocryphal books is fixed; no new books or writings are added. By contrast, Pseudepigrapha keep appearing; one striking collection is that among the scrolls found in caves by the Dead Sea. So there are far more Pseudepigrapha than Apocrypha.

The Apocrypha were largely written for Jews, and to begin with they were highly regarded in Palestinian Judaism. Only later did 'apocryphal' acquire the meaning 'excluded from the canon', and therefore became a pejorative term.

# 3 Mishnah

## (a) Origins

The fact that in the time of Ezra the Torah came to be regarded as the fundamental written law of the Jewish people was of far-reaching significance. The consequence was that the precepts of the Torah came to regulate and control every single aspect of everyday life. There was no way in which one could escape the Torah. It was authoritative in every connection: marriage laws, food laws, laws of purity, social laws, legal concepts.

Its divine character meant that no one was allowed either to deviate from it in any way or to introduce any changes. Even the scholars whose permanent occupation was to study its complex of regulations were not allowed to have personal, divergent opinions of their own. They could engage in the interpretation of the Law, and seek to adapt it to circumstances, but they always had to begin from one unswerving principle: the text is given by God and cannot be altered by human minds.

However, there was one great difficulty. In the meantime the Torah no longer took into account the changing customs and circumstances of the Jews. Developments took place at this time, also, even if the pace was not as rapid as in our own day. So even then, it was clear that the Torah was not adapted to everyday life, and that was the occasion for the composition of the Mishnah.

This Mishnah goes back to two traditions. First, to the Torah, the law given by God on Sinai to Moses, in Hebrew called the Torah *shebiḥtau*, the written law. Large groups within orthodox Judaism believed that in addition to this there was also oral teaching, the Torah *shebe'al peh*, which was also revealed to Moses on Sinai, and handed down by him to the Israelite elders. Both traditions were equally sacred. Together, they form the basis for the Mishnah.

Schools were formed, in which rabbis and their pupils steeped themselves in the text of the Torah and the oral teaching from morning till night. Because it was forbidden to write down the texts of the oral teaching, for generations these discussions and the conclusions arising from them were always passed down by word of mouth. It may sound incredible to us, but it fits the whole pattern of that time.

One example may perhaps make clear the sort of question that had to be discussed. The Torah says, 'You may not work on the sabbath.' But what is 'working'? Something may be 'work' in some circumstances, but not in others. So how is work to be defined? Are there circumstances in which work is permissible or even necessary? Hundreds of regulations had to be discussed in this way; it was necessary to investigate possibilities in order to be able to make new regulations.

There were also areas of legislation in which the Torah made no provisions, or which had not been defined sufficiently clearly. Some practices had to be abolished because they had lost all meaning.

The Tannaim (scribes) also began to introduce certain laws. The marriage contract, the so-called *ketubah*, dates from this period. In it the husband accepts certain obligations, and the wife is given material protection should her husband die. A great deal of material came into being in this way; originally it was handed down orally, but eventually it was written down, and later called the Mishnah.

Although it is not clear what the real basis for the prohibition was, as I have already pointed out, there was a strict taboo against putting down the texts of oral teaching in writing. Perhaps the prohibition was meant more to prevent the circulation of these texts, should they be written down, than to prevent this writing in the first place. Perhaps there was a fear that the texts might be used or interpreted wrongly; the structure was still rather fragile. This distinguished the Jews from surrounding nations, which is perhaps in itself an explanation of this phenomenon.

It seems probable that the increasing influence of the New Testament in the second century AD helped to convince the Jews that they too needed to write down their oral tradition in order to avoid the possibility that less authoritative commentaries might influence the interpretation of the Old Testament.

However, various rabbis used the material which they had

collected purely as study material in their own schools. Such a collection was called a *mishnah* (teaching, teaching material), derived from the Hebrew verb *shanah*, which means 'learn, repeat'. The study of this material was made by scholars who were called Tannaim.

Rabbinic schools developed in many centres of Palestine at that time, under the direction of famous scholars, and these also influenced the character of this Mishnah. There were well-known schools in Lud (Lydda), Yavneh (Jamnia) and Tiberias, each with its own character.

People studied the Law theoretically, but there was also a great concern for casuistry, in other words the practical adaptation of the Law to everyday matters. This produced various tendencies, the influence of which was felt far outside the schools themselves. Conflicts over interpretation also increased, and this led to opposition against the views held by various schools. Presumably people were also doubtful about the authenticity of the sources with which they were occupied. In the last resort, they did not go back to an existing law book, but to traditional material, which had developed gradually as a result of the many additions to it. A split slowly began to come about between those who wanted to see the Torah *shebihtau* as the basis of the Mishnah and those who wanted to recognize both the Torah *shebihtau* and the second tradition, the Torah *shebe'al peh*, as the basis of the Mishnah.

Round about 200 BC this second tradition, that of oral teaching, was the occasion for the appearance of the two parties of Pharisees and Sadducees. The latter wanted to restrict themselves to the Torah, leaving aside the oral tradition based on it which was maintained by the Pharisees. However, study of the Mishnah remained central, to begin with only in Palestine, but from the beginning of the third century AD also in Babylonia.

## (b) The Soferim

The soferim are the earliest agents involved in handing down the tradition. Ezra was called *haSofer*, which is often translated 'the scribe'. Modern scholars think that this is incorrect, and that he must be thought of as 'the scholar, the one who could write and therefore had influence and importance'.

Important later representatives of the Soferim were the so-called five *zugoth* ('pairs'; singular *zug* = pair); these are teachers who were leaders of groups of Soferim from 160 BC onwards. They are said to have been in each case the *nasi* (the president) and the *ab bet din* (the head of the court) of the Sanhedrin. However, this too is now very much open to question. When the Great Assembly no longer functioned, an attempt was probably made to protect and preserve the Torah by means of the influence of the Soferim.

The five pairs were active from 160 BC to the beginning of the common era. They were:

1. Jose b. Joezer and Jose b. Johanan
2. Joshua b. Peraḥiah and Mattai of Arbela (not Nittai, as he is often called)
3. Judah b. Tabbai and Simeon b. Shetah
4. Shemaiah and Abtalion
5. Hillel and Shammai.

Hillel and Shammai are without doubt the best known teachers. They already had considerable authority during the reign of Herod (37–4 BC). Their views often clashed, in which case Hillel was always the more moderate. Their schools became famous, above all because the school of Hillel laid down a number of so-called 'derivative rules', according to which it is permissible to adapt regulations in the Torah by derivation and combination. Using these rules led, among other things, to a combination of the Torah *shebe'al peh* and the Torah *shebiḥtau*. To begin with, there were seven of these hermeneutical (from the Greek 'explain, expound') rules. Later, the number was extended to thirteen. First of all a general rule was established, a so-called *kelal* ('general'). A collection of rules was then built up on this, the so-called *halakoth*, which were learnt off by heart, and thus could always be easily adapted.

These rules were there to hand. One of the best-known derivative rules is that of the *kal wahomer*, which means, 'from the easy to the difficult'. This argues that there is all the more reason for drawing a particular conclusion. Here is an example. It is written, 'A man may not burden his enemy's ass to such a degree that he collapses under the load'. *Kal wahomer*, that means that a man should certainly not overload the ass of his friend.

## (c) The Sanhedrin

The word Sanhedrin is derived from the Greek *synedria*. This was a college of wise men, a kind of supreme council, in which the *nasi* (the president) and the *ab bet din* (the head of the court) were the leading figures. It had legal and executive power during the period of Greek and Roman rule. The tractate Sanhedrin in the Talmud mentions a Great Sanhedrin with seventy-one members and a lesser one with twenty-three members. According to the tradition, they were summoned by Moses and were an extension of the so-called *kenesset gedolah*, the great assembly, which is mentioned about 200 BC. (In modern Hebrew, the Knesset is the Israeli parliament.) The Sanhedrin is mentioned for the first time in 57 BC.

## (d) The Tannaim

After the Soferim come the six generations of Tannaim (scholars). Their activity extends from the beginning of the common era to 220. (Strack gives five generations, but he divides the second generation into an older and a younger group.) It was under their direction that the Mishnah came into being and was completed.

First of all comes the famous rabbi Johanan b. Zakkai, who lived in the first century AD and belonged to the first generation of the Tannaim. He was a pupil of Hillel and the founder of the legendary school in Yavneh (the Greek Jamnia), on the site of the modern Israeli kibbutz of Yavneh, south of Tel Aviv. The significance of this school as a centre of Talmudic study was further increased by the fact that it took over the role of the Sanhedrin when this council lost its original form after the fall of the Temple in AD 70. During the time of Johanan b. Zakkai, the ordination of rabbis by the laying on of hands was also introduced. This is the significance of the Hebrew 'obtain *semikah*', which means that someone has the authority of a rabbi as the result of the laying on of hands. This handing down of tradition could only take place in Palestine, and certainly was in force round about AD 350.

The Tannaim made various collections of *mishnah*. Every rabbi and his school had their own collection, which was studied and discussed at length. One famous collection is that of Rabbi Aqiba

(c. 50–135), from the second generation of the Tannaim; another is that of Rabbi Meir, one of his disciples who belonged to the fourth generation (110–175).

Another pupil of Rabbi Aqiba, who contributed a great deal to the formation of Midrash literature, is Rabbi Simeon b. Joḥai of the fourth generation (100–160?).

Beyond question, the final redactor of the Mishnah was Rabbi Judah haNasi. He was born in 135, the great-grandson of Gamaliel I, and lived until 217. His mishnah became what we call *the* Mishnah. The last generation of the Tannaim came to an end with his death.

In the Babylonian period the title rabbi ('my master'), which was given to scholars who came from Palestine, was replaced by rab ('master'). This is used exclusively for scholars coming from Babylonia.

### (e) The language of the Mishnah

The Hebrew of the Mishnah is sometimes called neo-Hebrew; that should not be confused with contemporary, modern Hebrew (*ibrit*) as it is spoken in Israel. In fact it is preferable to speak of Mishnaic Hebrew, because this distinguishes it better from biblical Hebrew – which was spoken from the beginnings of Hebrew as a language until about AD 200 – and later mediaeval Hebrew.

Mishnaic Hebrew was spoken and/or written from 400–300 BC to about AD 400. It was a living language, for everyday use, strongly influenced by Aramaic, which slowly but surely displaced it. When the Mishnah was completed round about AD 200, Mishnaic Hebrew had been almost completely suppressed as a spoken language. It was used only in the schools: first in Palestine, and later, when the Palestinian schools disappeared, in the Babylonian schools. However, by about AD 400 Mishnaic Hebrew had become a dead language. Mishnaic differs from classical, biblical Hebrew in both grammar and vocabulary. This is partly to be explained by the fact that during the time when the Mishnah was being composed, Hebrew had partly been displaced as a spoken language by Aramaic, which had become the vernacular. Words appear in the Mishnah which do not occur in the Bible, and vice versa. Sometimes the words in the Mishnah have acquired a meaning different from that which they had in the Bible.

25

This meaning often in fact goes back to the Aramaic. Because Hellenistic influence was also great at that time, a whole series of Greek and Latin loanwords have found their way into the Mishnah, some of which have returned in modern Hebrew. An amusing instance of this is the Greek *asemon*, which is a round coin without any inscription. In modern Hebrew, *asimon* is the word for a telephone token. The modern Hebrew *ambatyah* (bath) derives from the Greek *embate*, and the modern Hebrew *awir* (air) comes from the Greek *aer*.

The language of the Mishnah is generally clear. The text is written briefly and succinctly, and indicates that the judgments expressed were to be learnt off by heart. I have already said that the word Mishnah derives from the verb *shanah*, which in the first instance means 'repeat'. Consequently it went on to acquire the meaning 'learn', probably via the Aramaic. The connection between repetition and learning is not difficult to explain. In Aramaic the verb *tana* or *tane* also has both these meanings.

The Mishnah is referred to in the Babylonian Talmud as *mish-natenu*, our Mishnah, as contrasted with other collections of *mish-nah*, which are called *mishnayoth*. In Aramaic, the terms used were *matnitin* for 'our Mishnah', and *matnita* or *baraita* for other Mishnaic collections. By contrast, in the Palastinian Talmud, 'our Mishnah' is simply called *matnita*.

(*f*) The divisions of the Mishnah

The composition of the Mishnah is as follows. There are six divisions, which in Hebrew are called *seder*. Each of these is sub-divided into tractates, called *masseket* (or in Aramaic *messek-ta*). There are about sixty-three of these. Each tractate is further divided into chapters, called *pereq*, which total 525; and each chapter is divided into paragraphs, which are in turn called *mishnah*. There are 4187 of them. Thus the whole book is called *the* Mishnah. The division and the arrangement of all the books mentioned was not always done very systematically. In those days the construction and editing of a book of this kind was still a new discipline! The content of some of the chapters does not always agree with the subject of the tractate in which they are discussed.

The six divisions are as follows:

I Zeraim ('Anything that is sown'). This contains regulations about agriculture and the contributions which must be set aside for the poor, the priests and the levites. It is divided into tractates as follows:

1. Berakoth ('Benedictions'). These are principally daily prayers, which are discussed in nine chapters.
2. Peah ('Corner'). This is the part of the field which must be left for the poor. Eight chapters (see Lev. 19.9; Deut. 24.19, etc.).
3. Demai ('That which is uncertain'). A discussion of crops of which it is doubtful whether or not tithes should be made. Seven chapters.
4. Kilaim ('Mixtures, crosses'). This deals with the crops, materials and animals which must not be crossed or mixed with one another. Nine chapters (see Lev. 19.19; Deut. 22.9, etc.).
5. Shebiith ('The seventh year'). In this year all the fields have to be left fallow. Ten chapters (see Ex. 23.11; Lev. 25.1; Deut. 15.1).
6. Terumoth ('Heave offerings', viz., those which are due to the priests). Eleven chapters (see Num. 18.8; Deut. 18.4).
7. Maaseroth ('Tithes'). A tithe has to be made of the produce of the field, to be given to the Levites. Five chapters (see Num. 18.21).
8. Maaser Sheni ('Second tithe'), which has to be made as an offering to the temple in Jerusalem. Five chapters (see Deut. 14.22).
9. Hallah ('Piece of bread, dough'), which must be given as an offering. Four chapters (see Num. 15.18).
10. Orlah (literally 'Uncut'); this refers to the fruits of a tree during the first three years after it has been planted. These are not to be plucked. Three chapters (see Lev. 19.23).
11. Bikkurim ('Firstfruits'), which must be brought to Jerusalem. Three chapters (see Deut. 26.1).

II Moed (literally 'Appointed time', at which something happens in accordance with the calendar). This contains the regulations about the festivals and special days in the year.

1. Shabbath. This discusses the many laws which apply to the sabbath. Twenty-four chapters.

2. Erubin ('Mixtures'). On the sabbath it is permitted to travel or to carry objects only within a certain distance. The tractate discusses how these limitations can be extended. Ten chapters.
3. Pesahim ('Passovers'). This discusses the many regulations relating to the feast of Passover. Ten chapters.
4. Sheqalim (literally 'Shekels'). This is an agricultural measure, an amount which must be paid per head for temple worship. Eight chapters (see Ex. 30.11).
5. Yoma ('The day': Aramaic). This is a discussion of the regulations for the Great Day of Atonement and temple worship on that day. Eight chapters.
6. Sukkah ('Booth, tabernacle'). Regulations about the Feast of Sukkoth, the Feast of Tabernacles. Five chapters (see Lev. 23; Num. 29; Deut. 16).
7. Betzah ('Egg'). This tractate is also called Yom Tob ('Feast day'). It begins with the word *betzah*, hence the name. It discusses all kinds of regulations about festivals. Five chapters.
8. Rosh haShanah ('New year festival'). The celebration of this day is discussed, as is the ascertaining of *rosh hodesh* (the day of the new moon). Four chapters (see Lev. 23; 24; Num. 29.1).
9. Taanith ('Fast day'). When should people fast? Four chapters.
10. Megillath ('Scroll'). Generally speaking, this means *the* Megillah, the scroll of the Book of Esther. This discusses regulations in connection with the reading of this scroll and the celebration of the Feast of Purim. Four chapters.
11. Moed Qatan (literally 'Lesser appointed time', 'Lesser feast'). These are the days between the feasts of Passover and Sukkoth in the so-called mid-festival days. They are not *yom tob* days, but special rules apply. Three chapters.
12. Hagigah ('Celebration of a festival'). The celebration of the three main festivals in the temple at Jerusalem is discussed at length. These are: Passover, Shabuoth (= Pentecost) and Sukkoth. Three chapters.

III Nashim ('Women'). This chiefly contains a discussion of the laws about marriage, marriage rights and divorce.

1. Yebamoth (literally 'Sisters-in-law'). This discusses levirate marriage and marriage practices which are forbidden. In Hebrew *yabam* means 'brother-in-law', and it is his duty to marry the widow of his deceased brother, if as yet there are no offspring. Sixteen chapters (see Deut. 25.5).

2. Ketuboth ('Marriage contracts'). In a Jewish marriage the contract between the bridal couple is very important. Thirteen chapters.

3. Nedarim ('Vows'). This discusses the difference between an oath, a promise, obligations to celibacy and their annulment. Eleven chapters.

4. Nazir ('The Nazirite'). There is an extensive discussion of the law of the Nazirate in Wayyiqra (Numbers) 6. This tractate deals with that. Nine chapters.

5. Gittin ('Bills of divorce'). An extended discussion of divorce as it is dealt with in Debarim (Deuteronomy) 24. 9 chapters.

6. Sotah ('The woman who is suspected of adultery'). The regulations in connection with such a woman are given at length in Wayyiqra (Numbers) 5.11f., and are discussed here. Nine chapters.

7. Qiddushin ('Betrothals'). All the laws about marriage and its enactment are discussed here. Four chapters.

IV Neziqin ('Damages')

1. Baba Qamma ('First gate'). Ten chapters. (Baba is Aramaic for gate.)

2. Baba Mezia ('Middle gate'). Ten chapters.

3. Baba Bathra ('Last gate'). Ten chapters. Neziqin is an important and extensive division, because it discusses civil and penal law. Numerous problems appear in it. Presumably to begin with Neziqin simply consisted of the first three tractates.

4. Sanhedrin ('Law court'). This discusses how a judicial body must be made up. Eleven chapters.

5. Makkoth ('Blows'). This deals with corporal punishment, *inter alia* in connection with false witness. Three chapters. It is probable that at one time Sanhedrin and Makkoth together formed one tractate.

6. Shebuoth ('Oaths', in connection with legal matters). Eight chapters (Lev. 5.4).
7. Eduyoth ('Testimonies'). This deals with a number of subjects, not all of which are connected with judicial matters and which therefore do not all belong in this tractate. Eight chapters.
8. Abodah Zarah ('idolatry'). Five chapters.
9. Aboth ('Fathers'). Known usually as Pirqe Aboth ('The sayings of the Fathers'). This discusses many statements about morality and wisdom. Six chapters.
10. Horayoth ('Instructions'). This discusses what must be done when a wrong decision has been made. Four chapters (see Lev. 4.13).

V Qodashim ('Holy things'). This discusses sacrificial laws and service in and for the Temple.

1. Zebahim ('Sacrifices', especially blood sacrifices). Thirteen chapters.
2. Menahoth ('Meal offerings', especially of grain and bread). Thirteen chapters.
3. Hullin ('Non-holy things'). Food laws and divergences in the feeding of animals which makes them unsuitable to use. Twelve chapters.
4. Bekoroth ('First-born', especially the first-born of cattle). Nine chapters.
5. Arakin ('Valuations'). Leviticus 27 discusses the fulfilment of oaths. Nine chapters.
6. Temurah ('Exchange', especially that of sacrificial animals). Regulations about sacrifices. Seven chapters.
7. Kerithoth ('Uprootings'). In thirty-six instances the Law has the punishment of 'uprooting' from the people. That is discussed at length here. Six chapters.
8. Meilah ('Sacrilege', especially in the misuse of consecrated objects). Six chapters (see Lev. 5.15; Num. 5.6).
9. Tamid ('Always'). Here derived from 'olath tamid ('daily offering'), which is the subject of this tractate. Seven chapters (see Ex. 29.38; Num. 28.3).
10. Middoth ('Measurements'). The organization of the Temple. Five chapters.

11. Qinnim ('Birds' nests'). Deals with the offering of birds. Three chapters (see Lev. 1.5, 12).

VI  Teharoth (or Tohoroth: 'Cleannesses'). This division discusses ritual impurity.

1. Kelim ('Subjects, things'). How can something become ritually unclean? Thirty chapters. (See, *inter alia*, Lev. 6.20; 11.32; Num. 19.14).
2. Oholoth ('Tents'). One cannot remain under the same roof as a dead body without special regulations. Eighteen chapters.
3. Negarim (literally 'Plagues'). Leprosy is meant here (Lev. 13.14). When someone is leprous; what places on the corpse can be touched; the purification of clergy, the house and the dead body itself. Fourteen chapters.
4. Parah ('Cow'). The ashes of a red cow are a means of purification (Num. 19). Twelve chapters.
5. Teharoth ('Cleannesses'). This is another discussion of ritual impurity. Ten chapters.
6. Miqwaoth ('Ritual baths'). The requirements which a ritual bath must fulfil. Ten chapters (see Lev. 14.8; 15.5).
7. Niddah ('Object of impurity'). Menstruating women, and women who have given birth, need to follow a number of special regulations, also in connection with their social life. Ten chapters (see Lev. 12 and 15).
8. Makshirin ('What makes things capable of defilement'). The tractate is also called Mashkim ('Liquids'). This is a discussion of liquids which make dry materials unclean when they come into contact with them. Six chapters (see Lev. 11.34).
9. Zabim ('Persons with fluxes'). This also applies to men who are unclean in the terms of Lev. 15. Five chapters.
10. Tebul Yom ('Immersion of the day'). This means that someone has already taken the ritual bath during the day, but must wait until sunset for his ritual purity to be complete. Four chapters (see Lev. 15.5).
11. Yadaim ('Hands'). The impurity of hands and how they can become clean. Four chapters.
12. Uqtzim ('Stalks'). This discusses how far particular fruits can become unclean through their stalks. Three chapters.

# 4 Tosefta

The word Tosefta means 'addition'. The work to which this
name is given is a collection of explanations and points of discussion made by Tannaim, which is very closely connected with
the Mishnah. The Tosefta often gives the name of Taanaim who
are anonymous in the Mishnah. Like the Mishnah, the Tosefta is
in six divisions, each of which is in turn sub-divided into tractates and chapters. Broadly speaking, this subdivision runs parallel to that of the Mishnah, with the exception of four tractates
which occur in the Mishnah, viz.: Aboth from the fourth part
and the tractates Tamid, Middoth and Qinnim in the fifth part.

The Tosefta is an independent work, so it is difficult to explain
why it came to be given the name Tosefta. Addition to what?
There are various opinions about this. According to some, the
Tosefta is the Palestinian version of the Mishnah (Zuckerman-
del); others, including Albeck, think that the authors of the
Babylonian Talmud were unaware of the existence of the Tosefta.
It is certain that at points where there are differences between
the views expressed in the Babylonian Talmud and those of the
Palestinian Talmud, the Tosefta always follows the Palestinian
Talmud. The Tosefta is probably a collection of the teaching of
Rabbi Nehemiah, who was a pupil of Rabbi Aqiba. The relation
between the Tosefta and the Mishnah is unclear. Some parts of
the Tosefta, which are called Baraitoth, are variants of passages
which occur in the Mishnah; others are not found anywhere in
the Mishnah. At all events, the Tosefta never became as popular
as the Mishnah, though it is as ancient, and deals with the same
subject. Perhaps the reason for this is that it is very much less
clearly written.

The first edition of the Tosefta printed was that of Alfasi, produced in Venice in 1521. The most important commentator on it was Samuel b. Avigdor, who was also called Tanna Tosefa 'a.

To illustrate the difference between the Mishnah and the Tosefta, here is a passage from each. I have chosen the first paragraph of the first chapter of the first tractate of the first division of the Mishnah, i.e. Berakoth, Seder Zeraim.

From what time in the evening may the Shema be recited? (For the reciting of the Shema, see Deut. 6.4–9; 11.13–21.) From the time when the priests enter [the temple] to eat their *terumah*. (The *terumah* is the 'heave-offering', that part of the harvest which the peasants must put aside for the priests; the priests underwent ritual purification before they ate the *terumah*, after sunset, see Lev. 22.7) until the end of the first watch (i.e. the first part of the night, which was divided into three watches, see Lam. 2.19). Thus R. Eliezer. But the Sages say: Until midnight. Rabban Gamaliel says: Until the rise of dawn (i.e. the whole night, see Judg. 19.25). His sons once returned [after midnight] from a wedding feast. They said to him, 'We have not recited the Shema.' He said to them, 'If the dawn has not risen you are [still] bound to recite it. Moreover, wherever the Sages prescribe "Until midnight", the duty of fulfilment lasts until the rise of dawn.' The duty of burning the fat pieces and the members [of the animal offerings] lasts until the rise of dawn; and for all [offerings] that must be consumed the same day, the duty lasts until the rise of dawn. Why then have the Sages said: Until midnight? To keep a man far from transgression.

In comparison, here is the equivalent passage from the Tosefta:

['From what time in the evening may the Shema be recited?'] From the moment when people go into [their houses] to partake of their meal on the eve of the sabbath. Thus Rabbi Meir. But the Sages say: From the moment that the priests have the right to eat their *terumah*. The sign for this is the appearance of the stars. And although it cannot be proved, this is what is meant in Nehemiah 4.15 (EVV 4.21): 'So we laboured at the work, and half of them held the spears from the break of dawn till the stars came out.'

# 5 Baraita

The literal meaning of the Aramaic word *baraita*, plural *baraitoth*, is 'standing outside'. These are pronouncements of Tannaim which have not found a place in the Mishnah. Repeated reference is made to them in the Babylonian Talmud. A *baraita* is introduced in a specific way by the words *teno rabbanan*, viz., the rabbis have taught: *tanya*, *tena*, viz., it is taught. A great many of these *baraitoth* can be found in the Talmud. They are to be regarded as *halakoth* (see p. 60) standing outside the Mishnah.

The word *baraita* also occurs in the name of particular collections, viz., the Baraita of Rabbi Adda, which discusses matters concerned with the calendar; the Baraita of Rabbi Eliezer, better known under the name Pirqe de Rabbi Eliezer, dealing with the construction of the tabernacle; and the Baraita de Niddah, in which there is an extensive discussion of the laws of Lev. 15.19–33. The Tosefta is really a collection of *baraitoth*.

# 6  Gemara

We can understand how the Mishnah would become the object
of extensive discussions. All the notes of these discussions, and
all the reports made over the course of three centuries, were
collected together under the name Gemara, which also means
'teaching'. In modern Hebrew the verb *gamar* means 'end', 'fin-
ish', 'complete'. The Gemara is as it were a written commentary
or a report on the Mishnah. We might compare it with the
detailed minutes of a scholarly society. These great works, the
Mishnah and the Gemara, together form the Talmud. The word
Talmud also means 'teaching, study', from the Hebrew verb
*lamad* = learn. The name Gemara is of a late date; it was presumably introduced only as late as the Middle Ages.

So the Gemara has the function of a commentary and also a
supplement. The language of the Gemara varies: in the Babylonian Talmud, Hebrew and so-called East Aramaic is used. The
Jerusalem or Palestinian Talmud is written in Hebrew and West
Aramaic.

## (a) The Amoraim

The Amoraim were principally occupied in making commentaries
on the Mishnah. The word Amoraim means 'interpreters', from
the Hebrew verb, '*amar* = say. They were active from the third
to the sixth century AD. Hundreds of these Amoraim were at
work, over six generations; many of them enjoyed great authority. There was certainly regular contact between the Amoraim in
Babylonia and those in Persia. When the influence of the Amoraim in Palestine decreased considerably at the end of the fourth
century AD, the Amoraim in Babylonia came even more markedly
to the fore. This ran parallel to the great blossoming of spiritual
life among the Jews in Babylonia.

## (b) The thought-world of the Talmud

If we are to understand the origin of the Talmud, which is such an enormous work, we must know something about the conditions of the times and the milieu in which the Jews lived.

The text printed on the opposite page is a page from the Babylonian Talmud, the first page of the tractate Ketuboth: as we have just seen, Ketuboth is the second tractate of the third part of the Mishnah, viz. Nashim. This deals with legislation about marriages, and the laws and obligations existing between husband and wife once they are married. At a Jewish wedding the *ketubah* is given, i.e. a written marriage contract in which the husband declares which obligations he will fulfil. The word comes from the Hebrew verb *katab* = write. (The *ketubim* are the writings, which is the name of the last part of the Tanach.)

On the page reproduced opposite (the text is read from right to left), the text of the Mishnah begins in the box with the ornamentation: it is four lines long. After the two letters printed in bold type at the end of the fourth line, the Gemara text on this Mishnah begins. This text is much longer, because it goes at some length into the text of the Mishnah, which is presented in shortened form. We can see clearly how the views of the various rabbis were treated.

Commentaries on the Talmud are printed on the left and right of this central column; they mostly derive from the Middle Ages. In the text of the Talmud a small circle refers to passages in the Tanach which are connected with the subject; a small star refers to other passages in Talmudic literature.

The translation of the text of the Mishnah is as follows:

A virgin should be married on a Wednesday and a widow on a Thursday, for in towns the court sits twice in the week, on Mondays and on Thursdays; so that if the husband would lodge a virginity suit he may forthwith go in the morning to the court (Danby, p. 245).

Then follows the Gemara text, part of which may be translated as follows:

Rabbi Joseph says [that] Samuel says: Why did they (the Rabbis) say, 'A virgin should be married on a Wednesday'? Because we have learned: When the time has come [which is

36

בתולה

תנשאת ליום הרביעי אלמנה ליום החמש שפעמים בשבת בתי דינין יושבין בעירן ביום השני וביום החמישי שאם היה לו טענת בתולים היה משכים לבית דין: **גמ'** אמ' רב יוסף אמר רב יהודה אמר שמואל מפני מה אמרו בתולה נשאת ליום הרביעי לפי שאם היתה לו טענת בתולים היה משכים לבית דין...

appointed for the wedding] and they [the virgin and the widow] do not marry [because the husband fails to appear], then they [the virgin and the widow] eat of him [his food] and they eat of [his] *terumah* [if he is a priest].

It can be that if the time [of the wedding] occurs on the first day of the week, he has to give her something to eat. So we have learned: 'A virgin should be married on a Wednesday.' Rabbi Joseph said, O God of Abraham, he [Samuel] attaches a mishnah which is taught to a mishnah which is not taught. What was taught and what was not? The one was taught and the other was not. But [think of it in this way]: He attaches a mishnah which is explained to a mishnah which is not. [The discussion is concerned with the mishnah about going to the court early in the morning.] But as it is said [by Samuel], so we find: Rabbi Judah says [that] Samuel says: Why do they say, 'A virgin should be married on a Wednesday?' Because if he had a complaint about her virginity, he could go to the court early in the morning. Suppose they marry on Sunday: if he then had a complaint about her virginity, he could go to the court early in the morning [of the following day]. [Answer]: The Sages safeguarded the interests of the daughters of Israel, so that he [the bridegroom] should work for the [marriage] feast for three days, on Sunday, on Monday and on Tuesday, and on Wednesday he marries her. And now we have learned, 'they watch over her', we have also learned, 'If the time comes and they are not married, they eat of him [his food] and they eat the *terumah*' [in other words], that if the day is on Sunday, because he cannot marry [her because of the ordinance] he does not give her any food [on the three days mentioned, the Sunday, the Monday and the Tuesday]. Therefore [as Rabbi Joseph says]: If he is sick, or if she is sick, or if she is unclean [because of menstruation], he does not give her any food.

This translation gives us a clear indication of the way in which the scholars who produced the Talmud thought. All the words in square brackets do not appear in the Talmud, but they must be supplied if we are to follow the train of thought. Furthermore, it is now clear why the Gemara has such an extended text in comparison with the Mishnah. Every detail is subject to a new discussion and commentary.

# 7  Talmud

The Talmud should be regarded as a collection of commentaries, discussions, supplements and observations relating to the Mishnah. To get to know the Talmud calls for long and intensive study of this gigantic collection of material. It is necessary to become familiar with the associative way of thinking which is characteristic of the Talmud. One scholar says something, another scholar questions it, there is a discussion; then another quotation is introduced which is sometimes relevant to the subject being discussed and sometimes not. In this way the discussion moves from one topic to another. All the points made in these discussions were noted down over the generations, and this material forms the Talmud. The Talmud often also includes informal comments given as it were in passing, which makes the material even more extensive. Sometimes rabbis return to observations at a later stage and develop them further. There is no systematic framework to the Talmud; it forms a somewhat untidy collection and one needs to know one's way around it very well to be able to find the points which relate to a particular subject. The division is not schematic, and the names of the tractates do not really give adequate help in identifying their contents. The discussion of a particular problem is often to be found in a quite unexpected place.

The Talmud is not a law book. It does not contain any firmly prescribed rules; on the contrary, many conflicting views are evident. Rabbis often had quite different views on particular subjects. The character of the Talmud may best be described as discursive and expository.

Particular passages from the Talmud, taken completely out of context, are often used against the Jews. The Talmud has always been surrounded by a somewhat mysterious aura: it is the great secret book of the Jews, inaccessible to those who do not know the language. The great importance of the Talmud for the Jews is the way in which it gives a picture of the way in which rabbis worked over many generations, and the background information which goes with that. Because it contains statements on literally every facet of social and spiritual life, the Talmud has acquired great authority, and study of it is regarded as the greatest benefit for a Jew.

Education in the orthodox Jewish sense is not complete without a knowledge of the Talmud. Before the Second World War, in Eastern Europe children began to learn the Talmud when they were only four years old. Study of the Talmud still occupies a very important place in the teaching schools in Israel, the so-called *yeshiboth* (*yeshibah* means 'sitting').

The Palestinian or Jerusalem Talmud and the Babylonian Talmud came into being side by side. In Hebrew they are called the *talmud yerushalmi* and the *talmud babli*. There is considerable similarity in form and content; both the Palestinian Talmud and the Babylonian Talmud are very extensive works indeed, and to a large extent they correspond in content. The language in which they are written is different: the Jerusalem Talmud is written in Hebrew and West Aramaic; the Babylonian Talmud is written in Hebrew and East Aramaic. More Greek words have crept into the Jerusalem Talmud, and more Persian words into the Babylonian Talmud.

To begin with, the Jerusalem Talmud and the Babylonian Talmud enjoyed equal status. One was intended for the Jews in Palestine and the other for the Jews in Babylonia. With the decline of spiritual life among the Jews in Palestine, the Babylonian Talmud increasingly came into the foreground. The result of this is that when people now talk about *the* Talmud, they always mean the Babylonian Talmud. The authority of the Babylonian Talmud is also greater than that of the Jerusalem Talmud. In cases of doubt the former is decisive.

The Jerusalem Talmud is shorter than the Babylonian, perhaps because the formulations which it contains are more compact. The Jerusalem Talmud was presumably put together in haste as the situation in Palestine steadily became worse. As a result, many sentences are completed badly or not at all, and are crowded together without any clear indication of their subject-matter.

Nor are there references to the sources of remarks made in discussions, as there are in the Babylonian Talmud. The differences in content, along with the large degree of agreement, are a reflection of the different conditions under which the Jews lived in Palestine and in Babylon. However, there is no difference in principle between the two Talmudim as far as their methods of working are concerned. Both are markedly reflective and explanatory: dialectic plays a dominant role.

## (a) The Palestinian Talmud

Both the Palestinian and the Babylonian Talmud have only partial gemara on the tractates of the Mishnah. The Palestinian Talmud has gemara on all the tractates of the first three parts of the Mishnah. The fourth part is complete with the exception of Eduyoth and Aboth, while there are no gemara for Qodashim and Teharoth, with the exception of one tractate, Niddah. Perhaps there were once gemara which have then been lost. All in all, thirty-nine tractates out of sixty-three have gemara. There is no complete commentary on the Palestinian Talmud of the quality of Rashi's commentary on the Babylonian Talmud. The best-known commentaries date from the eighteenth century, e.g. that of Margolis. However, they cannot be compared with the commentary by Rashi.

The first edition of the Palestinian Talmud comes from Venice (1522). All the important commentaries are included in the Vilna edition of 1922. The only complete manuscript of the Palestinian Talmud known to us is in the possession of the University Library at Leiden.

## (b) The Babylonian Talmud

The Babylonian Talmud contains gemara on thirty-six tractates, of the first division only on Berakoth. There are gemara on all the second part with the exception of Sheqalim; on all of the third part; on all of the fourth part with the exception of Eduyoth and Aboth; on all of the fifth part with the exception of Middoth and Qinnim, and of the sixth part only on Niddah. A schematic survey of the two Talmudim is given in the table which follows.

The most complete manuscript of this Talmud is a

fourteenth-century codex now in Munich, which has been reproduced many times. One well-known version is the Vilna edition of 1902, which has been regularly reprinted. At present a new Soncino edition is being published in England with a translation; ten volumes have so far appeared out of a planned thirty-six. It will be some time before the edition is complete. A complete edition of the Talmud is being published in Jerusalem, edited by A. Steinsalz, with a critical apparatus. This edition, too, will not be completed for a long time. The first Babylonian Talmud was printed in 1484 at Soncino (near Milan), but it never amounted to a complete edition.

## (c) The divisions of the Talmud

| Division | Tractate | Numbers of chapters | Gemara in | |
| --- | --- | --- | --- | --- |
| | | | Palestinian Talmud | Babylonian Talmud |
| Zeraim | Berakoth | 9 | x | x |
| | Peah | 8 | x | |
| | Demai | 7 | x | |
| | Kilaim | 9 | x | |
| | Shebiith | 10 | x | |
| | Terumoth | 11 | x | |
| | Maaseroth | 5 | x | |
| | Maaser Sheni | 5 | x | |
| | Hallah | 4 | x | |
| | Orlah | 3 | x | |
| | Bikkurim | 3 | x | |
| Moed | Shabbath | 24 | x | x |
| | Erubin | 10 | x | x |
| | Pesahim | 10 | x | x |
| | Sheqalim | 8 | x | |
| | Yoma | 8 | x | x |
| | Sukkah | 5 | x | x |
| | Betzah | 5 | x | x |
| | Rosh haShanah | 4 | x | x |
| | Taanith | 4 | x | x |
| | Megillah | 4 | x | x |
| | Moed Qatan | 3 | x | x |
| | Hagigah | 3 | x | x |

| Nashim | Yebamoth | 16 | x | x |
| --- | --- | --- | --- | --- |
| | Ketuboth | 13 | x | x |
| | Nedarim | 11 | x | x |
| | Nazir | 9 | x | x |
| | Gittin | 9 | x | x |
| | Sotah | 9 | x | x |
| | Qiddushin | 4 | x | x |
| | | | | |
| Neziqin | Baba Qamma | 10 | x | x |
| | Baba Mezia | 10 | x | x |
| | Baba Bathra | 10 | x | x |
| | Sanhedrin | 11 | x | x |
| | Makkoth | 3 | x | x |
| | Shebuoth | 8 | x | x |
| | Eduyoth | 8 | x | x |
| | Abodah Zarah | 5 | x | x |
| | Aboth | 5 | | |
| | Horayoth | 3 | x | x |
| | | | | |
| Qodashim | Zebahim | 14 | | x |
| | Menahoth | 13 | | x |
| | Hullin | 12 | | x |
| | Bekoroth | 9 | | x |
| | Arakin | 9 | | x |
| | Temurah | 7 | | x |
| | Kerithoth | 6 | | x |
| | Meilah | 6 | | x |
| | Tamid | 7 | x | |
| | Middoth | 5 | | |
| | Qinnim | 3 | | |
| | | | | |
| Teharoth | Kelim | 30 | | |
| (also Tohoroth) | Oholoth | 18 | | |
| | Negaim | 14 | | |
| | Parah | 12 | | |
| | Teharoth | 10 | | |
| | Miqwaoth | 10 | | |
| | Niddah | 10 | x | x |
| | Makshirin | 6 | | |
| | Zabim | 5 | | |
| | Tebul Yom | 4 | | |
| | Yadaim | 4 | | |
| | Uqtzim | 3 | | |

## (d) The Jews in Palestine

We have virtually no certain knowledge about those who compiled the Jerusalem Talmud.

There were four important schools in Palestine. One was in Tiberias, led by Rabbi Johanan until his death in 279. After that, his pupils continued the school for a few years more. There were also schools in Lud (Lydda), Caesarea and Sepphoris. The earliest school was closed in the middle of the third century; the other three were closed in the middle of the fourth century by order of the Greek rulers. At that time there was an urgent need to consolidate and set down in writing all the material that had been collected in these schools. The Palestinian Talmud must have been finished about the end of the fourth century or the beginning of the fifth. Rabbi Jose b. Abin is often mentioned as a possible redactor; he belonged to the fifth generation of the Amoraim.

## (e) The Jews in Babylon

In 538 BC, Cyrus, the Persian king, had given the Jews permission to return to Palestine. Officially this marked the end of the Babylonian captivity. However, only a few Jews took advantage of this opportunity to return home. Most of them preferred to live in Babylon. Under Roman rule in Palestine, an increasing number of Jews emigrated to Babylonia, so that in some cities they amounted to a significant percentage of the population. Many Jews also went to other places, for example to Alexandria. The great Jewish communities in Egypt, which came to an end after the establishment of the state of Israel in 1948, derive from this time. The Jewish community flourished greatly in Babylonia. They enjoyed freedom of religion and political peace. At their head they had a ruler of their own, the Resh Galutah, an Aramaic title meaning 'head of exiles': the Greek term is exilarch. These exilarchs lived like kings, and had just about as much power. They were said to be descendants of David and inherited 'the throne'. Many writers claim that the last exilarch was Hezekiah, who lived in the eleventh century AD. On the other hand, it is assumed by others that the figure of the Resh Galutah certainly continued down to the thirteenth century AD. A similar figure was also to be found in the Jewish communities in Egypt, which I have already mentioned. Round about the seventh century AD, the power of the Resh Galutah came up against that of the Geonim (Gaon = 'pride', 'excellence'). These were the intellectual leaders of the time. Their influence extended down to the eleventh century AD.

In Babylon the Jews enjoyed a period of great prosperity, during which the production of literature also developed. Study of the Mishnah was carried on in the Babylonian schools under the direction of the pupils of the great Tannaim, who had brought the Mishnah, now complete, to Babylonia.

### (i) The Amoraim

The Amoraim in particular had great influence between the third and the sixth centuries. The more the schools in Palestine declined, the more those in Babylon thrived. The leading schools were those of Sura, founded in 219 by Rab, who was really called Abba Arika. (Rabbis in Babylon were no longer called 'Rabbi', but 'Rab'.) Rab died in 247. Meanwhile, a school had been founded in Nehardea by the scholar Samuel, who died in 254. Both were pupils of the great Rabbi Judah haNasi, the final redactor of the Mishnah; they made their school very famous. After the destruction of Nehardea in 259, the school was moved to Pumbedita. There, instruction was given by Rabba b. Nahmani (who died in 330); his successor was Rab Joseph, who in turn was succeeded by Abaye, who was succeeded by Raba. The discussions between these last two form an important part of the jurisprudence which also bears their names, viz. Ḥawayoth de Abaye weRaba. Raba moved the school from Pumbedita to Maḥoza on the Tigris. Six generations of Amoraim worked at these schools in the period down to the year 500.

The famous Rab Ashi worked in Sura from 375 to 424. He played a very important part in the final redaction of the Talmud. During the time that he was in charge, the assemblies which were held twice a year in the month preceding the great festivals (i.e. March and September), the so-called Kalla (the etymology is unknown), were very well attended. One particular tractate of the Mishnah was studied in detail at these meetings and a commentary on it was produced. All the points which had been discussed earlier by the Rabbis were discussed again. The aim of

Rab Ashi was to revise existing material, which had already become very extensive, and to put it in order. Year after year he had this vast amount of material discussed and developed in this way by his pupils and their audience, so that in the end they could put it in some order. To a large extent his work of redaction can be found in the Talmud as we now know it. The finishing touch was put to the Talmud by the successors of the Amoraim, the Saboraim ('those who reflected', viz. on the material).

The Saboraim were active only for a short period, from the end of the fifth century until the middle of the sixth. They were probably the ones who completed the Talmud.

### (ii) The Geonim

After the Amoraim, leadership of the schools was taken over by the Geonim, who were able to maintain this high intellectual standard (apart from a short break) down to the eleventh century. The school of Sura had its last period of prosperity at the time of the leadership of Saadya, who was appointed in 928 (see p. 65). After his death in 942 the school was closed for a while, but it was opened again in 987. In 1038 this famous school finally came to an end, and with it an important period in the spiritual life of the Jews. Sherira (968–998) worked at the school of Pumbedita. He was succeeded by his son Rabbi Hai (939–1038), who brought to this school a final period of prosperity during which students came to Pumbedita from many lands. After 1038, the two schools were combined, and continued for another 150 years in Baghdad.

The Geonim were regarded as the supreme authorities on spiritual matters. (In the secular sphere the supreme authority was the Resh Galutah.) Their knowledge of the Talmud was enormous, and because of this they made numerous decisions which were necessary for everyday life. They were not just teachers, but functioned as lawyers who interpreted the Law when constantly changing circumstances made that necessary. Their decisions were binding on all Jewish communities. They often received questions about particular religious or social problems, which they answered with extensive quotations from scripture. These Responsa, called She'eloth uTeshuboth (questions and answers) in Hebrew, form an extensive corpus of material which gives us some insight into the conditions and problems of this period (see pp. 71f.). The Geonim were also the first to send messengers to remote communities to keep them up to date with the latest commentaries on the Talmud.

Finally, mention must also be made of the important contribution of the Geonim in the sphere of liturgy and prayer. The first complete prayer books known to us were both compiled by Geonim: Amram Gaon (856–874) compiled the Siddur Rab Amram, and Saadya Gaon the Siddur Saadya Gaon. This was intended especially for Jews in Egypt.

## Summary

| Soferim | From 200 BC to the beginning of the Christian era. |
| Tannaim | From the beginning of the Christian era to 220. |
| Amoraim | From 220 to about 500. |
| Saboraim | From 500 to about 650. |
| Geonim | From 650 to 1050. |

# 8 The Minor Tractates of the Talmud

At the end of the fourth part of the Babylonian Talmud, the Seder Neziqin, we find a number of *massektoth ketanoth*, the so-called Minor Tractates. The number of these Minor Tractates varies in the different editions of the Talmud. There are fifteen of them in the Vilna-Romm edition. They must be regarded as a series of tractates which for one reason or another were not included in the Talmud. Strack also calls them the extra-canonical tractates. It is not clear whether these tractates were deliberately excluded from the Talmud on the orders of Rabbi Judah haNasi, the final editor of the Mishnah, or whether they had not yet been composed at the time when the Talmud was completed, towards the end of the fifth century. Furthermore, we do not know with any certainty when they were composed. A complete edition of these Minor Tractates appeared in England in 1965, along with a translation (Soncino). The largest tractate is the Aboth de Rabbi Nathan, which is really an expansion of Pirqe Aboth. The second tractate is Kalla Rabbathi, which must be regarded as a gemara on Kalla. Zunz calls the other thirteen Minor Tractates, 'baraitoth in the form and style of the Tosefta'. They are: Soferim, Semaḥot, Kalla, Derek Erez Rabba, Derek Erez Zuta, Pereq haShalom, Gerim, Kuthim, Abadim, Sefer Torah, Tephillin, Zizith, Mezuzah.

The tractate Aboth de Rabbi Nathan, which is also called the Baraita of Rabbi Nathan, is ascribed to Rabbi Nathan haBabli, a man born in Babylonia, who migrated to Palestine in the middle of the second century. His father was the exilarch in Babylonia: he himself was a learned man who was appointed, along with Rabbi Meir, as head of the Bet Din, the court of justice, in Palestine. As a result of deep-seated differences of opinion with the patriarch of Palestine, at that time Simon ben Gamaliel, the two of them tried to depose the patriarch from office. When their attempt was discovered, they themselves were removed from office, but later they were readmitted on condition that their names should never be mentioned in connection with decisions of a halakic kind. The decisions of Rabbi Meir are therefore said to be concealed behind the introductory words 'Others say', and those of Rabbi Nathan behind the words 'Someone says'. This will explain why the final redactor of the Mishnah, Rabbi Judah haNasi, who was the son of Simon b. Gamaliel, kept the name of Rabbi Nathan out of the Mishnah. However, it is known that Rabbi Nathan compiled a Mishnah and a Baraita on his own account. So it is perfectly possible that this tractate comes either from him or his school, though there are also those who would dispute this.

# 9  Midrash

The word is derived from the Hebrew verb *darash*, which has different meanings. In modern Hebrew it means 'demand', 'require'. As far as we are concerned here, it means 'investigate', 'expound', 'explain'. The independent noun *midrash* is derived from this, and means exposition or explanation.

This word has become a technical term for the exposition and explanation of passages from the Tanach, the Mishnah and the Talmud.

There are two ways in which the text can be approached:

1. Through the *peshat* (= simple). This is the direct or, one might say, simple explanation of a word or passage. The interpreter does not look for anything behind the text. This is called the objective method.

2. Through the *derash*, the investigating method, which is also called the subjective method. The *derash* must adapt a particular text or passage to the changes of everyday life. If this could not be done directly, the interpreter began to read a particular meaning into the text or into a word in order to obviate the difficulty.

This gave rise to the Midrash, and the schools where this study was practised are called bet haMidrash. The midrash became an extremely important component of Talmudic study. The method was probably already adopted by certain sects which lived round the Dead Sea.

There are special reasons for the great importance of the Midrash. The captivity in Babylon forced the Torah well into the background. Ezra did a great deal to restore the Torah to the centre of Jewish life. When the Jews returned to Palestine, under Ezra and Nehemiah the study of the Torah again became very important, and the following of the laws which it contained was no less so. When the Temple was destroyed in AD 70, the Torah was the only spiritual possession of the Jews. The Mishnah and the Talmud only came much later. However, it was not possible to make direct use of the Torah for daily living. A great deal had to be done to adapt the laws to a pattern of life which had undergone change in the meanwhile. In order to provide an ongoing interpretation of already existing laws, which were formulated quite briefly, the laws were adapted and made suitable. This came about by the system of midrash, interpretation and explanation. The law which emerged from this was the Midrash Halakah, much of which found a place in the Mishnah.

Another form of midrash appeared later, the Midrash Haggadah, narrative Midrash. The Tannaim used midrash a good deal, so that the material constantly grew.

Once the Midrash Halakah had been incorporated into the Mishnah, Midrash simply meant Haggadah. This was then further divided, so that *the* Midrash related to books of the Tanach, and was real explanatory midrash, while *the* Haggadah related to non-biblical books. The latter chiefly consisted of sayings, legends and popular stories: narrative midrashim.

Haggadah occurs in both the Palestinian Talmud and the Babylonian Talmud, but the most important collections of midrash are quite independent. There are the following collections.

## (a) Midrash Rabbah

This title is reserved for a collection of Haggadic literature which simply consists of midrashim on the five books of the Torah and the five Megilloth (= scrolls).

Consequently we find mention of:

    Bereshith Rabbah
    Shemoth Rabbah
    Wayyiqra Rabbah
    Bemidbar Rabbah
    Debarim Rabbah
    Ruth Rabbah
    Esther Rabbah
    Shir haShirim Rabbah
    Qoheleth Rabbah
    Ekah Rabba.

This collection of Midrashim appeared at various times, but they probably cover a period of about a thousand years, viz., from the Tannaim down to the tenth century. The two examples below will give a clear idea of the markedly associative character of these Midrashim. We might call the thought-patterns pre-logical, most similar to the patterns of the unconscious. Many of us are so conditioned to rational thought-patterns that we wrongly tend to undervalue these other thought-patterns.

By way of illustration, here are two extracts. The first is a fragment from Bereshith Rabbah 17.5–8, relating to Bereshith (Genesis 2.21; compare it with Rashi's interpretation on pp. 66f. below).

5. 'So the Lord God caused a deep sleep to fall upon the man, and while he slept took up one of his ribs and closed up its place with flesh.'

Rabbi Joshua of Sikinin says in the name of Rabbi Levi: Sleep is the beginning of man's downfall: if he is sleeping, he is not sitting to study or working. Rab says: There are three kinds of stupor: the stupor of sleep, the stupor of prophecy and the stupor of the unconscious. The stupor of sleep: this is evident from 'And then God caused a deep sleep to fall upon man' (Bereshith 2.21). The stupor of prophecy is evident from: 'As the sun was going down, a deep sleep fell on Abram' (Bereshith 15.12). The stupor of the unconscious is evident from: 'No man saw it, or knew it, nor did any awake; for they were all asleep, because a deep sleep from the Lord had fallen upon them' (I Samuel 26.12). The rabbis say: There is also the stupor of folly, for it is written: 'For the Lord has poured out upon you a spirit of deep sleep' (Isaiah 29.10). Rabbi Haninah b. Isaac says: There are three things that are incomplete. Sleep is the incomplete experience of death; the dream is an incomplete form of prophecy; the sabbath is the incomplete form of the world to come. Rabbi Abin adds: There are two more: the bowl of the sun is an incomplete form of the light from above, and the Torah is an incomplete form of the wisdom from above.

6. 'Then he took one of his ribs [sides] . . .' Rabbi Samuel b. Nahman says: He took one of his sides, for it is written: 'And for the second side of the tabernacle on the north side'

(Shemoth 26.20). But Samuel maintains: He took one rib from between two ribs, for it does not say [he filled] *its* place [with flesh], but [he filled] *their* place [with flesh].

7. A Roman woman once asked Rabbi Jose: Why [is woman made] by theft? He replied to her: Imagine that someone secretly leaves an ounce of silver with you and you openly give him back a pound. Is that theft? She said to him, 'But why secretly?' He replied: First he made her for him, and he saw that she was filled with blood. He took her from him, returned, and made her for him the second time. Then she said, 'Now I can understand. I was given in marriage to my mother's brother, and because I had grown up with him in the same house, I became ugly in his eyes. He went away and married another woman who was not as attractive as I. Moreover, there was once a pious man who married a pious woman. They had no children and said to each other, "We are no use at all to God." They arranged a divorce. He married a godless woman and she made him godless; she married a godless man and made him pious. So you see, it all depends on the woman.'

The second is a fragment from the Midrash Ekah Rabbah I, 16.51, relating to Ekah 1.16. The verse discussed is: 'For these things I weep, my eyes flow with tears, for a comforter is far from me, one to revive my courage' (Ekah 1.16). (This is about the birth of the Messiah.) There now follows a discussion between Rabbi Abba b. Kahana and Rabbi Joshua b. Levi about the name of the comforter. Rabbi Judah then says in the name of Rabbi Aibu: His name is Menahem, that is, the comforter, because I can relate the following story:

There was a Jew who went ploughing. An Arab came past, whereupon his ox began to low. The Arab said to him, 'Jew, son of a Jew, loosen your ox, loosen your yoke, loosen your plough, because the Temple is destroyed.' He asked, 'How do you know that?' He said, 'Because your ox is lowing.' The Jew loosened his ox [which is regarded as a sign of mourning], he loosened the yoke, he loosened the plough. While they were talking together, the ox lowed for the second time. The Arab said to him, 'Son of a Jew, make fast your ox, make fast your yoke, make fast your plough, because the Messiah is born.' He said to him, 'Where is he born?' He replied, 'In the city of

53

Bethlehem in Judah.' He said to him, 'What is he called?' He said, 'Menahem [the one who gives comfort].' He asked him, 'Whose son is he?' He said, 'Hezekiah's.' He sold his ox, he sold his plough and he bought children's clothes. He travelled from one city to another and from one province to another until he arrived at Bethlehem in Judah. And when he arrived in Bethlehem in Judah, all the women came up to him and he tried to sell them clothes for their children. He said to them, 'Which of you is the mother of Menahem?' They said to him, 'The one over there.' But while all the other women bought clothes for their children, she did not. He asked her, 'Why are you not buying clothes for your son Menahem?' She said to him, 'Because there is an evil omen upon my child. When he was born, the temple was destroyed.' He said to her, 'Let us hope that the temple was destroyed in his footsteps, so it shall also be rebuilt.' And he said to her, 'Buy clothes, and if you have no money, I will give them to you.' And so it came to pass. After a few days he thought, 'I must go and see how things are faring with the child.' He came to the woman and asked, 'How is it with your child?' She replied, 'Did I not tell you from the moment that you came that his omen is evil? There is even an evil omen upon his soul. A strong wind has come and blown him away, and I do not know where he has gone.' He said to her, 'Did I not say that when he was born [the temple] was destroyed and that it will be rebuilt on his return?'

Rabbi Aibu says, 'Why must I hear this from an Arab when there is a text which clearly states, "And Lebanon shall fall through the mighty one" (Isaiah 10.34)?'

## (b) The Tannaitic Midrashim

These comprise a large number of midrashim which are very old and come from the time of the Tannaim, who are repeatedly mentioned in them. However, the Amoraim were presumably the final redactors. These midrashim include both halakic and haggadic material, and are written in Hebrew, with a few Greek words.

This kind of midrashic collection exists for Exodus, Leviticus, Numbers and Deuteronomy. There was probably never such a collection for Genesis. The collection of midrashim on Exodus is called the Mekilta, Aramaic for 'measure, form'. This book is often called the Mekilta de Rabbi Ishmael (*c.* 60–140), because it was traditionally accepted that he was its editor. He and his pupils are often mentioned in it. The Mekilta may originally have been formed of two collections, which have been brought together. It is striking that Tannaim are mentioned by name in the Mekilta who remain anonymous elsewhere in midrashic literature.

The Mekilta is divided into nine tractates, which are in turn sub-divided into sections. It is one of the earliest collections made by the Tannaim, though it is not mentioned in the Talmud. The Amoraim were certainly aware of the existence of this Mekilta. When there is a difference of opinion between the Babylonian and the Palestinian Talmud, the Mekilta follows the latter.

The first printed version of the Mekilta dates from 1515 (Constantinople), the second from 1545 (Venice). The best-known translation into English is that of Lauterbach (1933). We now know of the existence of yet another Mekilta, that of Rabbi Simon b. Johai. In content this Mekilta corresponds closely to that of Rabbi Ishmael. To begin with, this Mekilta was well known, but it disappeared after the sixteenth century; however, at least part of it has been reconstructed by means of the discoveries in the Cairo Geniza. The most complete edition is that by Epstein and Melamed (1955).

The Sifra ('the book'). This collection of midrashim on Leviticus is also called the Sifra debe Rab ('The book of the house of the master'), or Torath Kohanim ('The law of the priests'). The book owes its name to the fact that in the schools, studies often began with the book of Leviticus. There is a good deal of disagreement over the authorship of the Sifra. It, too, is a collection of halakic and haggadic material which is divided into fourteen sections, in turn sub-divided into chapters and paragraphs. The halakic element is predominant. The first edition appeared in Constantinople in 1552, the second in Venice in 1645. The first commentator was Abraham Ibn Daud, surnamed Rabad (for this form of abbreviation see above, p. 1). There is no usable translation of the book. The Sifra is attributed to the school of Rabbi Aqiba.

The Sifre (Aramaic for Hebrew *sefarim* = books) is a collection of midrashim on Numbers and Deuteronomy. The collection comes from two different schools: that on Numbers was made by pupils of Rabbi Ishmael, and that on Deuteronomy was made by pupils of Rabbi Aqiba. Probably the collection on Numbers is earlier than that on Deuteronomy.

There should have been another Sifre on Numbers. Fragments of it are included in the Yalqut haShimeoni on Numbers. (Yalqut means collection.) This is called the Sofre Zuta (Aramaic for 'the little books'). It probably derives from the school of Rabbi Simon. We also come across this book under the names *midrash shel panim aherim* (the midrash from the other perspective). The Sifre is also divided into sections. The earliest edition appeared in Venice in 1545.

The Midrash haGadol ('The Great Midrash') is a thirteenth-century work from the Yemen. Modern scholars feel certain that the author was David b. Amram Adani. The manuscript was discovered only in the nineteenth century.

This collection of midrash is particularly important because the author provides a great deal of information about the life of the Jews in the Yemen. He has also included and worked over a great many pieces of midrash which were later lost. Incomplete and unknown collections of midrash can be studied more easily by means of this Midrash haGadol. Schechter, for example, was able to include some of this collection in his Aboth de Rabbi Nathan (1887). The reconstruction of the Mekilta de Simon b. Johai was also made largely by means of this collection.

Quite apart from the ten books of the Midrash Rabbah, there are also numerous other midrashim. One great collection of midrash can be found in the Tanḥuma. All the stories here begin with the words: *yelammedenu rabbenu* ('Our Rabbi, teach us'). Then there are also midrashim which have a special connection with festivals. They are usually called Pesiqtoth. Well-known collections are the Pesiqta de Rab Kahana and the Pesiqta Rabbati. The Aboth de Rabbi Nathan, which I have already mentioned earlier, really belongs in this category, as do some of the other Minor Tractates (see pp. 48f.). Then there are also the Seder haOlam and the Pirqe de Rabbi Eliezer, which contain stories connected with creation.

The Yalqut haShime'oni was arranged in the thirteenth century; this includes a good deal of midrash material like the Yalqut haMakiri and the Midrash haGadol.

It is difficult to date all these collections of midrash because there is often uncertainty as to their authorship. They are divided into three different periods of composition: early, middle and late.

The table below gives only the most important collections of midrash, which I have already mentioned. It should not be forgotten that many other names could be added.

| | | |
|---|---|---|
| Bereshith Rabbah | 400–500 | early period |
| Wayyiqra Rabbah | | |
| Ekah Rabbah | | |
| Esther Rabbah | | |
| Pesiqta de Rab Kahana | 500–640 | |
| Ruth Rabbah | | |
| Shir haShirim Rabbah | | |
| Qoheleth Rabbah | 640–900 | middle period |
| The Tanḥuma | 775–900 | |
| Yalqut haShime'oni | c. 1250 | |
| Yalqut haMakiri | c. 1350 | late period |
| Midrash haGadol | | |

# 10  Halakah

The word *halakah* is derived from the Hebrew verb *halak*, which means 'go, follow'. Halakah thus means literally 'going, following', but it has acquired the figurative sense of the law or the regulation that one follows, the religious Law. In the singular it also means 'the Law', the normative part of the Torah, and in particular oral teaching. In the plural one speaks of halakoth, which then means a collection of laws, rules of behaviour.

Tradition attributes the origin of the halakah to Moses, because people talk about the halakah leMoshe miSinai, i.e. the Law which was given to Moses on Sinai. This halakah is very old and does not find any support in the Torah, in contrast to the Midrash, whose concern it is in fact to establish the connection between the law and a biblical text or passage.

How does a law become halakah? There are a number of criteria for this, which in principle are built up from five elements. This halakah must come from one of the following five sources:

1. The Torah (the written teaching)
2. Tradition as this appears in other books of the Tanach (prophets and writings)
3. Oral teaching
4. Rulings of the Sages
5. Custom.

A law or precept can become halakah through all these channels. The first three elements are called 'deOraita', i.e. a halakah which is based on the Torah. The last two are called deRabbanan, i.e. deriving from the rabbis. The halakah which is mentioned under 3. as coming from oral teaching is sub-divided into the halakah miSinai and the halakah leMoshe miSinai. The latter term is used for halakoth which have no points of contact in the Torah.

The development of the halakah can be described in general terms as follows. The halakic rules already existing had to be made to agree with the text of the Torah. Presumably the collection of halakic rules was already begun in about 200 BC. In the apocryphal book of Jubilees, which was produced about 150 BC, we find halakic rules. It is generally assumed that these are rules which were made by the Pharisees. The conflict between the Pharisees and the Sadducees plays an important role in the development of the halakah at about this time. The Pharisees were ready to accept oral teaching; the Sadducees kept exclusively to written teaching. There was probably a concern to strengthen the position of the Pharisees over against that of the Sadducees by means of the creation of the halakah. (The third sect which was in being at the same time, that of the Essenes, probably had little influence on the final redaction of the halakah.)

The starting point was thus the fact that a great deal of authority was attached to the Torah. The adaptation of the rules was made in accordance with the principle of *derash*, the explanatory, expository method, of which the midrash is the result.

This led to a binding law, which people tried to systematize. The halakah had to be adapted and applied to everyday life, and in this connection there was a need for short and succinct formulations. As time went on, the original text which had formed the starting point was gradually allowed to fade into the background, so that the halakah came to be detached from the broader midrashic element.

In the earliest stage, Midrash halakah and Midrash haggadah were closely intertwined. The Midrash haggadah does not go back to the biblical texts, but explains the biblical narratives by brief stories and sayings. The brief formulations of the halakah now led to the Mishnah, a collection of halakoth which contains hardly any haggadah.

Various Tannaim had their own collections of halakoth, which were regularly handed on. The most famous collections were those of Rabbi Meir, Rabbi Judah, Rabbi Jose and Rabbi Simon. The Midrash began to have a life of its own and became the source of study, by means of an extensive midrashic literature.

## (a) Codification

The halakah was more or less complete round about AD 200. This was principally the work of the Tannaim. The addition of new rules, halakoth, remained possible in the case of a hitherto unprecedented situation. Changes could no longer be introduced.

A number of codices of halakoth appeared, like the Halakoth Gedoloth ('The great halakoth') a systematic arrangement of all the laws which appear in the Talmud. This book was created in the eighth century, in Babylon. The first edition dates from 1548 (Venice). The Halakoth Ketsuboth ('The established halakoth') is primarily a discussion of laws which arose after the Torah, chiefly in the period of the Geonim (650–1050). For the discussion of other codifications, see pp. 69ff.

## (b) Significance

The significance of the halakah for orthodox Judaism is enormous. It is the foundation for Jewish life. All laws and regulations from the Torah are incorporated and discussed in it, and it is no more permissible to deviate even a hair's breadth from the halakah than it is to deviate a hair's breadth from the Torah. The halakah protects orthodox Judaism from outside influences, and even now fulfils the function that people wanted to give to it: the protection of Jewish religion and the practical adaptation of the Torah to all situations which can arise in everyday life with its changing phenomena (think of electricity!). Hence we find a casuistry which never has an end.

# 11  Haggadah

The word haggadah derives from the Hebrew word meaning narration. This is that part of oral tradition which relates stories, legends and sayings of the wise men and the prophets. It does not deal with the Law, or with laws, far less does it give any kind of explanation why the laws or the commandments were given. Haggadah can appear in many forms: stories, parables, allegories, proverbial descriptions, laments, words of comfort, metaphors and plays on words. However, the starting-point always remains faith in God and the way in which this must come about. Haggadah is often difficult to read, because times and places are often confused. It also has popular stories which can no longer be directly connected with biblical accounts. Haggadah is concerned with the problems of life, creation, the function of man in creation, his relation to God and the universe, the problem of good and evil, and the place of Israel among the nations. It also contains reflections on a future life. Haggadah also discusses the political and social circumstances of the various periods in which particular scholars lived.

Parts of the Talmud are composed of haggadic material, interspersed with halakic material. Haggadah was influenced by the circumstances of the periods in which the Talmud was compiled. The Tannaim probably themselves already began to arrange the haggadic narratives; the first editions of haggadic stories only appeared at the end of the tenth century. This is very extensive material, popular because of the simplicity with which it is expressed.

The great Hebrew poet Haim Naḥman Bialik (1873–1934) popularized haggadah by his collection, the famous Sefer haAggada ('Book of the Haggadah'). In systematic fashion, he classified an enormous amount of haggadic material by subject and content. The time when haggadah was composed is not of primary importance, nor are the authors. The time of its origin must be regarded as a long period, 'the epoch of the haggadah', and the authors included in the collection are to be seen as 'the creators of the haggadah'.

Bialik's book has become an authoritative anthology which reflects the character of haggadah in a distinctive way. I have added two passages in translation to give some idea of the characteristic thought-patterns of haggadah.

On the relationship between a person and their surroundings.
A man must not remain awake among those who are asleep and must not sleep among those who are awake.
He must not lament among those who laugh nor laugh among those who lament.
He must not sit while others are standing nor stand when others are sitting.
He must not read [from the Torah] while others are teaching [from the Mishnah] and he must not teach while others are reading.
The moral of this story: a man must not behave differently from his fellow-men.


About a person's house.
This is the story of a maid who went to her father's house. She was pretty, and wore jewellery of gold and silver. She lost her way and went on without stopping. Because it was already the middle of the day, she became thirsty, but she had no water. Then she saw a well and a rope from a bucket which was stuck fast in it. She took the rope, divided it into three pieces and went down into the well. When she had drunk, she tried to get out again, but was unable to. She began to lament and to shout. Then a young man came along, and he heard her. He stopped by the well and looked at her. He said to her, 'Who are you? Are you a human being or a spirit?' She said, 'I am a human being.' He said to her, 'Who are you?' She told him the whole story. He said to her, 'If I get you out, will you marry me?' She replied, 'Yes', and he hauled her up. He tried to have sexual intercourse with her. She said to him, 'From which people do you come?' He replied, 'I am from Israel and

I come from this particular place and I am a priest.' She said to him, 'God has chosen you and sanctified you from all Israel and you try to behave like a beast, without *ketubah* [marriage contract] and without wedding vows. Come with me to my father and mother, because they are from such a family, noble and esteemed in Israel, and I will marry you.' They pledged their troth one to another. Then she said, 'Who is the witness?' A rat came past. Then she said, 'This rat and this well are witnesses in the case.' And each went their way. The maid kept her promise; when anyone asked anything of her she refused, and when they seized her she behaved like someone suffering from epilepsy, and tore her clothes and those of anyone else who touched her, until people kept away from her. And he arrived in his own city, broke his promise and married another woman. He had two sons; one of them fell into a well and died, and the other was bitten by a rat and died. Then his wife said, 'How has it come about that our two sons should have died in such a strange way?' He told her what had happened. She asked for a divorce and said to him, 'Go to the portion that God has given you.' He went to her city and there asked after her. They told him, 'She is suffering from epilepsy. If anyone touches her she does this and that to them.' He went to her father, and explained the whole story and said to him, 'I accept any fault that she has.' He appointed witnesses in the matter. He came to her. She began to behave as she had become accustomed. He told her the story of the rat and the well. She said to him, 'I have remained as I promised.' And immediately her spirit became calm and she married him. And they had sons and many possessions. And about her the psalmist says, 'I will look with favour on the faithful in the land' (Ps. 101.6).

# 12   Mediaeval Rabbinic Literature

Round about the tenth century, after Babylonia and Persia had ceased to be the spiritual centre for the Jews, Jewish culture flourished greatly in Spain. This success later spread to northern and southern France and the Rhineland (Worms). At that time Spain was Islamic, and Arab culture was already highly developed. The result of this was that Jewish scholars in Spain not only knew Hebrew and Aramaic, but also had a thorough knowledge of Arabic. For the first time in history, a Hebrew philology developed which was based above all on a comparative study of the three languages mentioned. Grammar was studied systematically, and this led to a modern form of biblical exposition. The two basic principles on which the exegesis of the Bible and the Talmud had hitherto been based were, as we have already seen, (*a*), the *peshat*, the most simple and direct approach to the word or the text, and (*b*) the *derash*, the explanatory, expository method which was always concerned with something behind the text. The Midrash developed from this (see p. 50 above).

Now commentators began to make use of comparative philology; furthermore, their view of the world was rather different from that of the Tannaim and the Amoraim. The influence exercised by these commentators was enormous. The whole of modern biblical scholarship still makes continual use of their commentaries. In addition to this contribution in the form of commentaries, mediaeval rabbinic literature gave an impetus to the rise of the so-called codices and the response literature. The beginnings of this can already be found at the time of the Geonim, but this form of literature now developed fully. Numerous commentators, collectors of codices and scholars were at work from the tenth century on, to begin with in Spain, and later in northern and southern France, the Rhineland and Italy. They carried on an extensive correspondence in the form of questions and answers (*she'eloth uteshuboth*).

## (*a*) Commentators

I shall mention here the most important of the dozens of scholars who lived in the Spanish period and have left behind this work in Hebrew and/or Arabic.

Saadya Gaon (Saadya b. Joseph) was not born in Spain, but in Fiume in Egypt (882–942). From 922 he worked in Babylonia. He had a great knowledge of Arabic and devoted himself to a systematic study of Hebrew grammar in comparison with Arabic. He translated the Tanach into Arabic, wrote an important philosophical work in Arabic called Amanat wal-I'tiqadat, which translated into Hebrew is *'emunoth wedi'oth* ('Beliefs and Opinions'). He also produced an Arabic grammar and numerous commentaries and wrote a good deal in Hebrew. His contribution to the liturgy has become well known because he compiled the first prayer book, the Siddur de Rabbi Saadya Gaon. He was one of the first to try to detach himself from the traditional method of interpreting the Tanach and the Talmud by the age-old patterns of the Midrash. He looked for an explanation by means of the comparative philology of Hebrew, Aramaic and Arabic. Because he had an outstanding knowledge of philosophy, his philosophical insights were also incorporated into his commentary.

The best-known commentator is without doubt Rashi, so named after the initial letters of his name: Rabbi Solomon b. Isaac. He lived from 1040–1105 in Troyes, France. Rashi performed the truly gigantic task of providing not only the whole of the Tanach but also the Talmud with a detailed commentary which is used even now by anyone who wants to study these books. Rashi always began from the simplest points and sought to explain the text in this way, without complicated additions. He introduces a good deal of midrashic literature into his explanation of the Tanach, but he gives it his own interpretation. Still, there is a notable difference between his commentary and that of, for example, Ibn Ezra. Perhaps one might say that while the Spanish Jews were trained scientists, because they had taken account of philosophy, astrology and medical science (Maimonides, see pp. 73f. below), Rashi was more the type of the Talmudic scholar in the classical sense, who arrived at his commentary by his formidable knowledge of the text and the language of the earliest sources. We may claim that his commentary on the Torah laid the basis for study by later generations. His commentary on the Talmud contributed much to the stabilization of the text, because he defined certain concepts. His corrections were incorporated in the editions of the Talmud which were printed later, and as such were of far-reaching influence.

The work of Rashi was continued by disciples of his school. They have come to be known as the Tosafists, because they wrote the Tosafoth (additions) to Rashi's commentary on the Talmud. The most famous disciples were his three sons-in-law, Rabbi Meir b. Samuel (c. 1060–c. 1135), Rabbi Samuel b. Meir, who was called Rashbam (the abbreviation of his full name: c. 1085–1160). The work of the Tosafists is often critical of the work of Rashi, and was carried on for a long time after his death by schools of Tosafists in Europe. Their work is always printed on the left hand side of the text of the Talmud, while that of Rashi is on the right.

As an illustration I have included a translation of Bereshith 2.20–23, followed by Rashi's comments.

20. The man gave names to all cattle, and to the birds of the air, and to every beast of the field; but for the man there was not found a helper fit for him.
21. So the Lord God caused a deep sleep to fall upon the man (Prov. 19.15), and while he slept he took one of his ribs and closed up its place with flesh.
22. And the rib which God had taken from the man he made into a woman and brought her to the man.
23. Then the man said, 'This at last is bone of my bones and flesh of my flesh. She shall be called *isshah* (woman) because she was taken out of man (*ish*).'

Rashi:
20. 'Everything to which man gave a name, living beings, etc.' . . . Turn the verse round and explain it as follows: Everything that lives and to which man has given a name must continue to be so called for ever . . .

21. 'So God caused a deep sleep to fall . . .' When he brought them, he brought them all before him two by two, male and female, and he said: 'All have a companion, and I alone do not'; then he immediately made sleep come upon him.

'From his sides' . . . From his sides, just as we find in Exodus 26.20 [of the tabernacle] or of the sides of the altar as in Exodus 27.7. That is what the Sages have said: two faces were made.

'He closed . . .' the place of the cut.

'While he slept he took' . . . so that he should not see the piece of flesh from which she was made and she should not therefore disclose her shame before him.

22. 'He made' . . . Like a structure which is broad below and narrow above in order to bear a child; like a granary which is broad below and narrow above so that it will not collapse under its weight.

'And he made the side into a woman' . . . that she should be a woman, as we find in Judges 8.27: Gideon made himself an ephod and placed it in his city of Ophrah. (An ephod is here a memorial stone.)

23. 'This at last' . . . That teaches us that man went among all animals, both tame and wild, and that he found no rest there. So now a woman has been made from the bone of one side, but a woman has not yet been made of the bone of one side.

'She shall be called *isshah*' . . . This is a play on words (*isshah* = woman from *ish* = man), and that is a sign that the world was created in [with] the holy language.

Another well-known commentator was Abraham Ibn Ezra (1089–1164), who lived for a long time in Spain and then travelled for a long time through Europe and perhaps also visited Palestine. He wrote a famous commentary on the Tanach. He had a great knowledge of Hebrew grammar, which he also discussed at some length and adapted to his explanations. As a philologist he had a critical approach to the text. He had also had a good philosophical training. He translated a great deal from Arabic into Hebrew. After that of Rashi, his was the most popular commentary on the Tanach.

The Kimḥis were a well-known group of commentators. The Kimḥi family consisted of the father, Joseph (*c.* 1105–1170), and two sons, David (*c.* 1160–1235) and Moses (the exact date of whose birth is unknown). They had a great knowledge of both Hebrew and Arabic grammar. Joseph Kimḥi wrote commentaries on the Tanach in which he devoted a good deal of attention to the grammatical aspects. In the grammar books which he wrote he introduced a division of the vowels into five long ones and five short ones.

David Kimḥi, called Redak, is the best known of the three. He wrote a book summarizing the research done in grammar and philology up to that time. His sefer haShorasim (Book of Roots, i.e. of a verb) is particularly well known. His influence was extensive because his commentaries, under the name Redak, were incorporated into the standard editions of the Hebrew Bible. As they were translated into Latin, they were subsequently taken over into many other translations of the Bible. In his method of interpreting the text he perhaps comes between Ibn Ezra, who has more of a philosophical approach, and Rashi, who tries to keep things as simple as possible.

Moses Kimḥi (Remak) was the author of the first printed edition of a Hebrew grammar (Soncino 1489). This book, *mahalak shewile ha-da'at* (= 'The Course of the Ways of Knowledge') was also translated into Latin and consequently became extremely important. His commentaries are less well known than those of Redak.

Finally, I must mention three other well-known commentators: Ramban, an abbreviation of Ṛabbi Ṃoses ḅ. Ṇaḥman (Naḥmanides), lived from 1194–1270. He was an exceptionally learned man, who like Maimonides was an artist, a philosopher, a rabbi and a Talmudic scholar. He wrote a philosophical work in which for the first time we can detect a mystical trend. At the end of his life, a theological dispute over his views led to his being exiled from Spain. He finished his famous commentary on the Torah after travelling to Palestine. He continued the work of Rashi and Ibn Ezra, but diverged from Rashi because of his marked mystical inclination.

Obadiah de Bertinoro (*c.* 1450–1510) was an Italian Talmudic scholar who later settled in Palestine. He wrote a well-known commentary on the Mishnah, which went into many editions and was also translated into Latin.

Isaac Abarbanel (Abravanel, 1437–1508) originally lived in Portugal where he served as a statesman. In addition to that he was a great Talmudic scholar and was well versed in philosophy. To begin with he fled to Spain, but in 1492 he went to Italy, and wrote his commentary on the Tanach in Venice. His commentaries were used a great deal in the seventeenth and eighteenth centuries by non-Jewish interpreters of the Bible, as the result of which they exercised great influence. They are less popular in Jewish circles than, for example, those of Rashi and Ibn Ezra, probably also because they are so long. Abarbanel also wrote a good deal in the philosophical sphere.

## (b) Codifications of the Talmud

From the end of the period of the Geonim, about the year 1000, the Talmud was regarded as a law book which governed every facet of Jewish life. Strikingly, however, it is not a real law book in which every statement has a particular validity. Many conflicting viewpoints are presented; there is much discussion of them, and the material is not arranged in a systematic way. It is very difficult to find all the passages dealing with a particular subject. The final conclusion about particular problems is often hidden under endless discussions.

It goes without saying that after the completion of the Talmud, a pressing need arose for a practical book, one that people could find their way around more quickly and in which they could find a conclusion without tedious searching. Law books of this kind have been compiled over different periods, based on the material in the Talmud. The earliest work is that of Alfasi, who died in Spain in 1103. He did not yet arrange the material according to subject, but shortened the Talmud considerably by omitting all the discussion which was not on the point. He limited himself to the halakah, i.e. to the laws, and did not include any haggadic material. He also omitted the halakic material which applied to the period before the destruction of the Temple.

The best-known work in this field is that of Maimonides (see pp. 73f. below), the so-called Mishneh Torah (repetition of the teaching). This work was composed about 1170. It was also called Yad Hazakah, which means 'strong hand'. The numerical value of the Hebrew letters *yod* and *daleth* (which together form the word *yad*) is fourteen, and that denotes the fourteen chapters of this famous work. Maimonides arranged the material according to subject-matter, and then divided it up in a more convenient way. The language in which he wrote this book was more akin to the Hebrew of the Mishnah, and was therefore easier to understand. Maimonides provided his own judgment in a number of passages, because often no judgment had been given in the Talmud. This course of action brought him a good deal of criticism from his contemporaries because they thought that he had moved too far from the original approach of the Talmud and the rise of the halakah. He was thought to want to interpret too much himself. However, this codex of Maimonides became very significant, because in their study of the Talmud later generations asked why Maimonides had made certain decisions in a particular way. He called his work Mishneh Torah ('repetition of the Torah') because he was of the opinion that it was now enough simply for someone to read the Torah and his book. For those who wanted to know the oral doctrine, the study of other books had become superfluous.

After the Mishneh Torah of Maimonides came the 'Arba a Turim ('The Four Rows') of Rabbi ben Asher, who died in Toledo in 1304. He wrote this codex, called the Tur for short, above all for Jews in countries outside Spain, because in his view Maimonides had applied himself too much to attitudes there. This codex was overtaken in popularity by two great and famous works by Joseph Karo (1488–1575), Beth Joseph ('The House of Joseph') and the Shulḥan 'Aruk ('Prepared Table'). Karo was probably born in Spain. After many travels he eventually arrived in Turkey, where he began his work Beth Joseph in 1522. He worked on it for thirty years from c. 1536 at Safed, in the north of Palestine.

In Safed, since the end of the fifteenth century, the Jewish community had grown to about 1000 Jews by the arrival of numerous immigrants from Spain and Portugal. Many preferred to go and live in Safed, where newcomers received a warmer welcome than in Jerusalem. So Safed developed into an important spiritual centre. Karo contributed a great deal to this development.

In his work Beth Joseph, Karo took up and explained the Tur of Asher at some length. As a result of his systematic and clear approach to the extensive and quite chaotic material, he soon came to be regarded as an extremely authoritative expert on the halakah. In 1555 he completed his second work, the famous Shulḥan ʿAruk. This much more succinct codex, which should be regarded as an extract from his Beth Joseph, became very authoritative and popular. In turn, additions and commentaries to this work, often very critical, appeared. The differing decisions of Rabbi Moses b. Isserles, surnamed Rema, are printed by each paragraph of the Shulhan ʿAruk. Not without wit, he called his commentary Mappaḥ ('Tablecloth'). He lived in Eastern Europe from 1525–1572. It is very understandable that an enormously large work like the Talmud is never accepted as it is and that commentaries and expositions on it constantly appear. The various codices which have appeared over the course of years have made the study of the Talmud easier, but they have never been able to take the place of the Talmud. For an orthodox Jew the Talmud is still always the source to draw on and the background against which attempts are made to answer contemporary questions.

### (c) Responsa (she'eloth uteshuboth)

The Geonim, who were the supreme authorities in the spiritual sphere until about the twelfth century, took many decisions in respect of the laws which appear in the Talmud. There was a constant need to interpret these laws in order to adapt them to everyday life, which was always subject to change. Because the authority of the Geonim was recognized by all Jewish communities, they regularly received questions from these communities, which they answered at length. Many of these answers developed into whole treatises on religious or social problems. The Geonim discussed numerous aspects of the law in this response literature. When their influence declined, this system of questions and answers continued, and has lasted down to the present. A rabbi receives a question about a religious problem and gives his answer by means of the literature available, with the support of the Talmud and the commentaries.

Over the course of the centuries this response literature developed into a gigantic body of material which gives an important insight into conditions in the Jewish world from about 900 to the present day. Numerous attempts have been made to arrange and publish this enormous material, inter alia in the Otzar haGeonim

(The Treasury of the Geonim) of B. M. Lewin. One modern edition is that of S. Freehof.

I have included below a very short fragment of an 'answer' given by Maimonides. It is taken from the collection of the Answers of Rambam (Maimonides), Teshuboth haRambam no. 42.

The proselyte (convert) asks:

Moses, the son of Rabbi Maimon, one of the exiles from Jerusalem who live in Spain, says: I have received the question from the wise and learned Obadiah, the proselyte. May God reward him for his work, the God of Israel under whose wings he has sought protection.

You ask whether during the praises which you say, by yourself or in the community, you may speak of '*Our* God and the God of *our* forefathers', or 'who has hallowed *us* by your commandments', or 'who has chosen *us*', 'who has led *us* out of Egypt'.

Yes, you must say all this in precisely this way, altering nothing, just as a Jew does, whether you pray by yourself or in the congregation, because Abraham had the true faith and taught the worship of God to all people. He abolished the worship of idols. He brought many men under the wings of the divine majesty and instructed them. So everyone who is converted to Judaism is counted a disciple of Abraham. Therefore you must pray, *Our* God and God of *our* forefathers, for Abraham is your father. And you must also pray, You, who entrusted the land to *our* forefathers, because it is written, 'For I have given it to you.' You may, of course, change the words 'God who brought *us* up out of Egypt' in your prayer, but you do not need to. There is no longer any difference between us and you. For it also says in Isaiah (56.3): Let not the stranger who comes to God say, 'God will certainly separate me from his people.' There is no difference between you and us in any single respect. And beyond doubt you must utter the blessing, 'who has chosen *us* and given *us* the Torah'. For you, too, have been chosen by the Creator. The Torah is given to us and to the proselytes. For it is written: there is one law for you and those who dwell as strangers in your midst (Numbers 15.5). Understand that when our forefathers went out of Egypt, they were idolaters. They had mingled there with the Gentiles, and had learned from their actions (Ps. 106.35). You must not underestimate your descent. For as we all come from Abraham, Isaac and Jacob, so too you come from the one who made this world. For Isaiah said (44.5): 'One shall say, I am of God, and the other shall call himself by the name of Jacob.' It is clear from all this that you must pray: *Our* forefathers were entrusted . . . and that Abraham is your father, as he is our father and father of all the righteous who walk in his ways. So you must not change anything in your prayers.'

## (d) Maimonides

Maimonides was called Rambam as an abbreviation of Rabbi Moses b. Maimon. He was born in Cordova in 1135 and died in Egypt in 1204. His family had to leave Spain about 1150. After living for some time in Morocco, Maimonides moved to Cairo in about 1170, where he was elected leader of the Jewish community. (His tomb is in Tiberias, in Israel, and many people go to visit it every year.) As well as being a rabbi, Maimonides was also an artist and a philosopher. To begin with, he wrote in Arabic, which was translated into Hebrew. His first commentary on the Mishnah was an Arabic commentary, Kitab as-Siraj, in Hebrew Sefer haMaor. The best-known parts of this are the introduction to the tractate Aboth, the Shemonah Peraqim ('The Eight Chapters'), and an introduction to the tenth chapter of the tractate Sanhedrin, Ḥelek. These two works began to lead a more or less independent life, because they were published separately, in view of the great importance that was attached to them. The introduction to Aboth has eight chapters discussing ideas in the sphere of the psychology of religion. The introduction to Sanhedrin leads to the formulation of the thirteen principles of Judaism. They are also called the thirteen rules of faith, because according to Maimonides, these ground rules must be accepted by all Jews. They presuppose that every Jew believes that:

1. God exists, as Creator;
2. God is one;
3. God is independent and does not have either form or shape;

4. God is eternal;
5. God is the only one in whom man must believe, and to whom man must pray;
6. It is necessary to believe in the prophetic books because of their divine character;
7. Moses is the greatest of all prophets;
8. The Torah was given to Moses on Sinai;
9. The Torah was given for ever;
10. God is omniscient;
11. There will be divine recompense in this world and in the world to come, in accordance with man's deeds;
12. The Messiah will come;
13. The resurrection of the dead will take place.

The synagogue of Fustat, near Cairo, where Maimonides was leader of the Jewish community, was built in 882 and later became famous. Since 1763 great quantities of manuscripts and parts of manuscripts have been found there, sometime loose pages, which have proved extremely important for the study of the Talmud, the history of those days, the liturgy and the Hebrew language. The manuscripts have come to light because of an earlier practice. It was the custom to hide away manuscripts which were no longer used, because holy books and writings might not be destroyed. In this Geniza (in Hebrew 'the place where something is hidden'), a great deal has been rediscovered. The same thing also happened much later (1947 and after) in the caves of Qumran on the west bank of the Dead Sea. The most important part of the Geniza treasures is in the possession of the University of Cambridge because in 1896 Solomon Schechter, at that time Reader in Talmudic at Cambridge University, more or less by chance caught sight of a few fragments which he immediately recognized as being very important. He was sent with all speed to Cairo and succeeded in bringing back bags full of fragments through diplomatic channels.

In about 1180 Maimonides' great work Mishneh Torah appeared. It has already been mentioned on pp. 69f. The first chapter of this book is also a philosophical treatise. The technical parts only appear later. 1190 saw the appearance of Maimonides' most famous work: Moreh Nebukim ('The Guide for the Perplexed'; Arabic Dalalat al-Ḥa'irin). This work was originally written in

Arabic. It was translated for the first time by Maimonides' friend Samuel ibn Tibbon in 1204 and later, in 1210, once again by Judah al-Ḥarizi.

The book consists of a philosophical approach to the principles of Jewish faith. Maimonides was strongly influenced by the philosophy of Aristotle (which was current in those days in intellectual circles), and his concern was to show that there was room for Judaism, as conceived of at that time, within Aristotelian thought-patterns. He tried to find a synthesis between science and faith. When, however, Maimonides went so far as to begin to regard the philosophy of Aristotle more or less as the basis on which Judaism had to be understood, he came up against a storm of protest in Jewish circles, above all when the translation of his work into Hebrew made it accessible to a wider public.

The scholars were divided into supporters and opponents of Maimonides, and taunts were exchanged fast and furiously. In Spain, Naḥmanides (see p. 68), who himself had a considerable philosophical training and was perhaps less far removed from Maimonides' approach (though he was certainly not one of his supporters), tried to arrive at a reconciliation. In France, the most prominent opponent of Maimonides was Gersonides, Rabbi Levi b. Gershon, surnamed Ralbag (1288–1334). He wrote a book, attacking Maimonides, called Milhamoth haShem (The Wars of God). However, the influence of Maimonides was enormous, above all in non-Jewish circles. His book was very carefully translated into Latin, so that it was read a great deal in scholarly circles. In 1305, a pupil of Naḥmanides, Rabbi Solomon b. Adret, resolved that the book should be read only by those above twenty-five years of age. However, in modern times there is no longer any opposition to the work of Maimonides, even in orthodox circles.

Here is a fragment from *The Guide for the Perplexed* III, 34.

On the significance of the Law
It is also important to note that the Law does not take into account exceptional circumstances; it is not based on conditions which rarely occur. Whatever the Law teaches, whether it be of an intellectual, a moral or a practical character, it is founded on that which is the rule and not on that which is the exception; it ignores the injury that might be caused to a single

person through a certain maxim or a certain divine precept. For the Law is a divine institution, and [to understand its operation] we must consider how in Nature the various forces produce benefits which are general, but in some solitary cases also cause injury.

We must consequently not be surprised when we find that the object of the Law does not fully appear in every individual; there must necessarily be people who are not perfected by the instruction of the Law, just as there are beings which do not receive from the specific forms of Nature all that they require. For all this comes from one God, is the result of one act; 'they are all given from one shepherd' (Ecclesiastes 12.11).

From this consideration it also follows that the laws cannot, like medicine, vary according to the different conditions of persons; whilst the cure of a person depends on his particular constitution at the particular time, the divine guidance contained in the Law must be certain and general, although it may be effective in some cases and ineffective in others. If Law depended on the varying conditions of man, it would be imperfect in its totality, each precept being left indefinite. For this reason it would not be right to make the fundamental principles of the Law dependent on a certain time or a certain place; on the contrary, the statutes and the judgments must be definite, unconditional and general, in accordance with the divine words, 'As for the congregation, one ordinance shall be for you and for the stranger' (translated by Friedländer, Routledge 1928, pp. 328f.).

# 13 Kabbalah

Kabbalah means tradition. Since the eleventh century there has been a mystical trend in Judaism, which goes directly to the books of the Tanach, where mystical desires and visions are already referred to. Mystical tendencies are also already present to a considerable degree in the Talmudic literature. They were principally grouped around the *ma'aseh bereshith* (the act of creation) and the *ma'aseh merkabah* (the work of the wheels). This is a reference to the divine wheels mentioned in Ezekiel 1.15. During the time of the Tannaim, the mystical trend of the *ma'aseh bereshith* was centred on the figure of Rabbi Aqiba, and that of the *ma'aseh merkabah* on Rabbi Johanan ben Zakkai. These mystical trends also existed in the time of the Geonim, in both Palestine and Babylonia. The Sefer Yetzirah probably came into being in Babylonia.

## (a) The Kabbalists

The Kabbalists can be divided into two main groups, the practical school, which was formed in the first half of the ninth century, principally in Germany, and the Franco-Spanish school, which flourished in Southern France and Spain from the twelfth to the fourteenth centuries. The practical school goes back to the mysticism of the time of the Geonim. The basic conception of the Kabbalah is that God is infinite, in Hebrew En-Soph. His Godhead is established by the ten *sephiroth*, perhaps best translated 'beings'. God himself is always beyond the comprehension of the human spirit. The *sephiroth* are: crown, wisdom, intelligence, loving-kindness, power, beauty, eternity, majesty, foundation and kingdom. The German school is represented by Judah ha-

Hasid ('The Pious'). He wrote the Sefer haHasidim ('The Book of the Pious') about 1200.

At the same time the Kabbalah reached Spain, with Gerona as a centre. Its practitioners formed a kind of secret society with a very elitist attitude. Nahmanides, the great Talmudic scholar, was one of them (see p. 68). His commentary on the Torah shows his mystical approach, which must be derived from the Kabbalah. Also as a result of his influence the Kabbalah spread to Provence, Italy and other European countries, and became enormously significant as teaching. Gershom Scholem, the great expert in Jewish mysticism, thinks that for anyone to want to explain the significance of the Kabbalah as a matter of chance is to show a complete lack of scholarly insight. When rabbinic Judaism increasingly began to lose influence, the Kabbalah was a decisive force on the life of the great majority. In his investigation of how the Kabbalah could become such an important and decisive factor, Scholem comes to the conclusion that this lies in the nature of its relationship to the spiritual heritage of rabbinic Judaism.

## (b) The Zohar

The earliest books of the Kabbalah are the Sefer haYetzirah, already mentioned earlier, and the Bahir, which appeared in Provence in the twelfth century. A new book, the Zohar, appeared about 1275. Its title means 'radiance', 'rays'. The book exercised a wide-ranging influence. It is written in the form of discussions which are said to have taken place in the second century between Rabbi Simon b. Johai and his pupils, at his school. The author gives free rein to his imagination and uses the Palestine of the time as a background. The whole work is composed as a Midrash on the Torah, Ruth and the Song of Songs. The author is verbose and constantly goes back to the principle of the ten sephiroth.

The name of Moses de Leon (who died in Spain in 1305) is associated with the Zohar, because in earlier literature he is often mentioned as the author of the Zohar. Scholem does not accept this. Such a view is no longer in accord with modern scholarship. In his view, here we have the compilation of a number of writings which were composed over a long period. The language of the

Zohar is a mixture of the East Aramaic of the Babylonian Talmud and the Aramaic of the Targum Onqelos.

Those who were forced to leave Spain in 1492 took the Zohar with them to their new abode, and so this book reached all the centres of Jewish life in Europe and strengthened the position of the Kabbalah. In Palestine, Safed became an important centre of Kabbalistic teaching and the Zohar. Because Rabbi Johanan b. Zakkai was buried near there, people felt a strong attraction to the place.

One of the most important figures of this period is Isaac Luria, surnamed haAri ('The Lion', 1514–1572). His contemporary Moses Cordovero, surnamed Ramak (1522–1570), wrote the Pardes Rimmonim in Safed. (The title means pomegranate orchard; in Modern Hebrew, a *pardes* is a pineapple plantation.) In it he discusses the relationship between the En-Soph and the sephiroth.

The relationship between the sabbath and the festivals on the one hand and the sephiroth on the other is an important point in the teaching of the Zohar. Every day stands under the sign of a sephirah; the sabbath stands under the highest sephirah, which as it were coordinates all the others (the malkuth). The sanctity of the sabbath casts its radiance on all the other days of the week. Thus we read in the Zohar:

> All six days of the transcendent world derive their blessing from the sabbath, and each supernatural day feeds the world beneath with what it receives from the sabbath (II, 88a).

The joy of the experience of the sabbath is identical with the experience of the sanctity of the sabbath. This exalted feeling is expressed in the hymn, written by Solomon al-Kabetz (1505–1572) which is still sung today every Friday evening in the synagogue as the sabbath begins: '*Leka dodi liqrat kala, pene shabbath nekabbela*.' 'Come, my friend, let us go to meet the bride, let us welcome the sabbath.' The metaphor is given material form in the symbol of the bride for the sabbath, for whom every Jew feels himself to be the bridegroom. Here magic has gone beyond the bounds of mysticism.

The zemiroth (singular zemirah = song) come from the same time; these are sung on Friday evening, and on the sabbath at mealtimes, to heighten the sabbath joy. From Luria comes the well known *Yom zeh leyisra'el ora wesimḥah*, 'This day is for Israel a light and a joy.' From his school also emerged the custom of singing the praise of the woman of the house on the Friday evening. At that time, the husband says the well-known words from Proverbs: *''eshet ḥayil mi yimtsa'?'*, 'A virtuous woman who shall find?'

From Safed the Kabbalah spread to other parts of Palestine and again to Europe. However, it was not until the rise of Hasidism in the eighteenth century that it had any influence on the mass of the people, in particular in Eastern European Judaism.

The most important figure of Hasidism, and its founder, was Rabbi Israel Baal Shem Tob, surnamed Besht (1700–1760). Baal Shem Tob means 'the owner of the good name'. Here the name means the name of God, because the word for God was not spoken. The pillars on which Hasidism rests are:

1. The text of Ps. 100.2: *'ibedu eth-hashem besimḥah bo'u lepanaw birnana* ('He in whom God delights comes joyfully before his face').

2. The worth of the Jew is not determined by his learning, but by his intention, his *hitlaḥawuth* (the modern Hebrew word *hitlaḥawuth* means enthusiasm).

3. Love for fellow man, the *'aḥawat yisrael*. This is literally 'love for Israel', but in those days contact with non-Jews was virtually non-existent. Love in the vertical sense is experienced on a horizontal level, so that the love of man for God becomes identical with the love of man for man.

4. The revaluation of man as the image of God. This had a powerful influence on the impoverished masses of East European Jewry.

In the course of its development, Hasidism fell apart into a number of sects, and small differences were blown up into breaking points. The most important sects are the Habad Hasidim, or the Lubavich Hasidim, coming from Lubavich in White Russia; the Gur Hasidim from Gur, and the Belz Hasidim from Belz, in the Ukraine, each with its own dynasty. Following the destruction of all Polish and Russian Hasidic centres during the Holocaust, new centres were established in Israel and in the United States.

The Hasidim observe strictly the precepts of the Torah. For them the performance of each commandment (*miṣwah*) is a means of obtaining *simḥah* (joy: *simḥah shel miṣwah* is 'the joy of the commandment'). The first pillar mentioned above (Ps. 100.2) is thus the *miṣwah shel simḥah* (the commandment of joy).

Martin Buber (1878–1965) made it his life work to integrate the Hasidic pattern of life and thought into a modern theology. However, the Hasidim themselves criticized him strongly, because in Buber's thinking there was little place for an orthodox, fundamentalist practice of religion.

# Bibliography

Albeck, C., *Mabo la-Mishnah* (Introduction to the Mishnah) (German translation: *Einführung in die Mischna*, Studia Judaica, ed. E. L. Ehrlich, Vol. VI, Berlin 1971)

Albeck, C., *Meḥqarim be-Baraita ve-Tosefta* (Studies in the Baraita and Tosefta), Jerusalem 1946, reprinted 1969

Altmann, A., et al., *Three Jewish Philosophers*, New York 1972

Bacher, W., *Die exegetische Terminologie der jüdischen Traditionsliteratur*, Darmstadt 1965

Bamberger, S., *Raschi Kommentar zum Pentateuch*, Basle 1962

Beek, M. A., *Aan Babylons Stromen*, Amsterdam 1955

– *Wegen en Voetsporen van het Oude Testament*, Baarn 1969

Ben Zwi, J., 'Keter ha-Tora shel Ben Asher she nichtab beyisra'el', *Sinai* 33, 1958, pp. 5ff.

Bialik, C. N., *Sefer ha-Aggada*, Tel Aviv 1962

Bloemendaal, W., *De tekst van het Oude Testament*, Baarn 1966

Bowker, J., *Jesus and the Pharisees*, Cambridge 1973

Charles, R. H. (ed.), *Apocrypha and Pseudepigrapha of the Old Testament*, Vols I and II, Oxford 1913

Davidson, I., Assaf., S., Joel, R. I. (eds.), *Siddur Rabbi Sa'adya Ga'on*, Jerusalem 1963

Dotan, A., *Dikduki ha Te'amim*, Jerusalem 1967

Eissfeldt, O., *The Old Testament. An Introduction*, Oxford 1965

Elliger, K., and Rudolph, W., *Biblia Hebraica Stuttgartensis*, Stuttgart 1976/77

Epstein, I., *Judaism*, Harmondsworth 1968

Epstein, N., and Melamed, E. Z., *Mekilta de Rabbi Simon ben Yohai*, Jerusalem 1955

Finkelstein, L., *Akiba, Scholar, Saint and Martyr*, New York 1970

Freehof, S., *The Responsa Literature*, Philadelphia 1955

– *A Treasury of Responsa*, Philadelphia 1963
– *Current Reform Responsa*, New York 1967
Ganfried, S., *Kitsur Sulhan Aruch*, Basle 1969
Ginsburg, D., *Introduction on the Massoretico-Critical Edition of the Hebrew Bible* (1897), with an introduction by H. M. Orlinsky, New York 1966
Ginzberg, L., *On Jewish Law and Lore*, New York 1970
– *Legends of the Bible*, Philadelphia 1972
Glatzer, N., *Maimonides. Ein Querschnitt durch sein Werk*, Cologne 1966
Goshen-Gottstein, M., *The Authenticity of the Aleppo Codex, Text and Language in Bible and Qumran*, Jerusalem 1960
Jakobovits, I., *Studies in Tora Judaism*, New York 1965
Jellicoe, S., *The Septuagint and Modern Study*, London 1968
Kadushin, M., *A Conceptual Approach to the Mekilta*, New York 1969
– *The Rabbinic Mind*, New York 1972
Kahane, A., *Ha-Sefarim ha-hitsonim*, Tel Aviv nd.
Kahle, P., *The Cairo Genizah*, Oxford 1959
Kittel, R., and Kahle, P. (eds.), *Biblia Hebraica*[3], Stuttgart 1937
Lauterbach, J. Z., *Midrash and Mishnah*, Philadelphia 1941
– *Rabbinic Essays*, New York 1951
Meijers, L. D. (ed.), *Chassidische Verhalen*, Baarn 1970
Melamed, E. Z., *Halachic Midrashim of the Tannaim in the Talmud Babli*, Jerusalem 1943
Metzger, B. M., *An Introduction to the Apocrypha*, London 1957
Mielzner, M., *Introduction to the Talmud*, New York 1968
Neusner, J., *The Life of Rabban Johanan ben Zakkai*, Studia Post-Biblica, ed. P. A. H. de Boer, Vol. VI, Leiden 1962
– *A History of the Jews in Babylonia*, Studia Post-Biblica, Vols. IX, XI, XII, XIV, XV, Leiden 1965
Newman, J., *Halachic Sources*, Pretoria Oriental Series, ed. A. van Selms, Vol. VIII, Leiden 1969
Oesterley, W. O. E., *An Introduction to the Books of the Apocrypha*, London 1946
– and Box, G. H., *A Short Survey of the Literature of Rabbinic and Mediaeval Judaism*, London 1920
Ploeg, J. van der, *Vondsten in de Woestijn van Juda*, Utrecht 1970 (with extensive bibliography)
Reisel, M., *Maimonides*, The Hague 1963

Roth, C., *A History of the Jews*, New York 1971

Rowley, H. H. (ed.), *The Old Testament and Modern Study*, London 1951

Russell, D. S., *Between the Testaments*, London and Philadelphia 1963

Scholem, G., *Major Trends in Jewish Mysticism*, London 1955 and New York 1972

Segal, M., *A Grammar of Mishnaic Hebrew*, Oxford 1970

Strack, J. L., *Introduction to the Talmud and Midrash*, New York 1963

Torrey, C. C., *The Apocryphal Literature: A Brief Survey*, New York 1960

Vries, B. de, *Hoofdlijnen en Motieven in de Ontwikkeling der Halacha*, Haarlem 1959

Vriezen, T. C., *De literatuur van Oud-Israel*, The Hague 1968

Weiner, H., *The Kabbala Today*, New York 1969

Winter, J., Sifra, *Halachischer Midrasch zu Leviticus*, Breslau 1938

Würthwein, E., *The Text of the Old Testament*, Grand Rapids, Mich. and London [2]1980

Zunz, J. L., *Ha Derashoth beYisra'el*, Jerusalem 1954

I have found the following editions useful in the study of the various books and writings discussed here:

*Kizzur Shulchan Aruch* (with a German translation), ed. S. Bamberger, Basle 1969

Maimonides, M., *The Guide for the Perplexed*, East and West Library, London 1952

*Mekilta* (English translation ed. J. Z. Lauterbach), Philadelphia 1933

*Midrash Rabba*, Hebrew edition with commentary by M. Mirkin, Tel Aviv 1956

*Midrash Rabba*, English translation with notes by the editors, H. Freedman and M. Simon, London 1939

*Mikra'oth Gedoloth*, Tel Aviv 1958

*The Mishnah*, Hebrew edition with commentary by C. Albeck, Jerusalem nd.

– English translation with introduction and notes by H. Danby, Oxford 1933

*Mishnayoth* (Hebrew with English translation by P. Blackman), London nd.

*Babylonian Talmud* (Hebrew with English translation), London 1971ff.

– (Hebrew only, with notes, ed. A. Steinsalz), Jerusalem 1968

*The Talmud* (English translation only), London 1938ff.

*The Minor Tractates of the Talmud* (with English translation), London 1965

*Tosefta* (in Hebrew, with introduction by M. Liebermann), New York 1958

*The Zohar* (with English translation by H. Sperling et al.), London 1934

*Zohar. The Book of Splendor*, ed. G. Scholem, New York 1971

# Index